Geek's Guide
to the
Wizarding World
of Harry Potter
at
Universal Orlando

2019 Edition

An Unofficial Guide for Wizards and Muggles

Mary deSilva

Cover Photo: Trevor Aydelotte
Book cover design inspired by Slytherin House

Books by Mary deSilva:

Fantastic Eats and Where to Find Them at Universal Orlando 2019

Universal Orlando Magic Tips 2019: Saving Time and Money and Universal Studios and Islands of Adventure

Universal Orlando Magic Tips 2017-Saving Time and Money at Universal Studios and Islands of Adventure

KIDS RULE! at Universal Orlando 2018

KIDS RULE! at Universal Orlando 2016

Geek's Guide to The Wizarding World of Harry Potter at Universal Orlando—A Guide for Wizards and Muggles

Universal Orlando Magic Tips 2016--Saving Time and Money at Universal Studios and Islands of Adventure

Escape from the Mousetrap 2016, Orlando Activities to Escape Walt Disney World

Universal Orlando Magic Tips 2015, Saving Time and Money at Universal Studios and Islands of Adventure

Escape from the Mousetrap 2015, Orlando Activities to Escape Walt Disney World

DEDICATION

For Lizzy

and

Kelly, Always

A portion of the proceeds from the sale of this book benefits Kelly C. O'Mahoney, Inc. in support of Brain Cancer Research. Go to KellyKickingCancer.org for more information.

CONTENTS

ACKNOWLEDGMENTS

My heartfelt thanks to several people for their help and encouragement in writing this, the fourth edition of this book. Thanks to Barbara Twardowski, my friend and travel writing mentor. Thanks to Susan O'Mahoney for listening to my ideas, offering unbiased critiques and editing.

Thanks to Trevor Aydelotte for his gorgeous cover photo of the dragon atop Gringotts.

Special thanks Kelly C. O'Mahoney. Her courage while battling brain cancer, gave me the courage to bring my travel writing ideas to reality.

I'd like to thank my family. Thanks to Jim for the many trips to Florida which inspired my ideas and for putting up with me while I got that last idea down on paper. Last but not least, thank you Patrick for encouraging me to read the Harry Potter books and Emily for being my Orlando buddy. Thanks sharing my enthusiasm and casting many spells with me.

LETTER TO THE WIZARDING AND MUGGLE COMMUNITY

Allow me to introduce myself. My name is Marianna Blackwater, born in the state of Florida and I am a witch of Native American descent. I have the title of Chief Witch of No-Maj* Relations, a division of The Magical Congress of the United States of America. Allow me to serve as your Magic Ambassador to the Wizarding World of Harry Potter at Universal Orlando Resort. This Muggle resort is located in the state of Florida, in an enchanted land called Orlando, which has been bewitching Muggles to visit and spend their currency since the year, 1971.

Many years ago, a clever wizard known as Walt Disney created his Muggle resort in Orlando but kept magic a thinly veiled secret. In 1971, he created a "Magic Kingdom" which featured magical attractions and fantastic beasts (flying elephants?). The new park was open to Muggles to visit and spend their Muggle currency. After the distinguished wizard passed away, the magic secret was kept by the wizards who followed, and his kingdom was expanded upon to attract Muggles from the world over. The creation of Magic Kingdom upset many in the magic community who felt that his "world" was in direct violation of the 1692 International Statute of Secrecy, which made it unlawful for magic to be performed in the presence of Muggles. After all, who would dispute the fact that his house elf, Mickey, was the inspiration for his most famous character, a talking mouse!

Years later in Great Britain, a clever witch called J. K. Rowling wrote a series of books chronicling the life of a young wizard, Harry Potter, "The boy who lived," famous for the defeat of "He who must not be named," the greatest dark wizard of all time. These books were made into films which made Ms. Rowling a very rich witch. She became very famous among Muggles (although many in the wizarding community speculate that she used the Confundus Curse on the Minister for Magic for allowing this blatant violation of the secrecy statute). These books gave Muggles another glimpse into the world of magic.

The books and subsequent films so enraptured such a great number of Muggles around the world, that they lead to a peculiar event in history. In 2010, the current Minister for Magic, Tarquin Littlefair, in an unprecedented move, gave a special waiver of the International Statute of Secrecy, and allowed the top wizards at Universal Orlando Resort to duplicate the Village of Hogsmeade and Hogwarts Castle. While the reasons for this move are highly debated, there is no question that the Universal Orlando wizards, using magic, created an uncanny version of Hogsmeade (I know, having visited the Scottish village myself twice). The result of the opening of Hogsmeade was that Muggles from all over the world flocked to the land of Orlando to see Hogwarts Castle, buy chocolate frogs, wands, wizard robes and other wizard trinkets.

In 2014, the savvy wizards at Universal Orlando again petitioned the Minister for Magic to extend the waiver to recreate Diagon Alley, (although it only took a few hours to create, the wizards used various charms to create the illusion of construction of Diagon Alley for two years prior to opening). In another unprecedented move, magical wands (called

Interactive Wands) were offered for sale at Ollivanders and other shops. While their power is limited, now Muggles can practice spell casting at many locations throughout Diagon Alley and Hogsmeade! Wizards of the Slytherin House protested the original plan for Diagon Alley and it was amended to include the addition of Knockturn Alley, an area focused on the dark arts.

What is next at Universal Orlando? The Dragon Challenge ride which was not really a wizard creation is gone and a new attraction is opening soon. We shall have to wait and see what the clever wizards at Universal Orlando have in store for us but speculations are that it will include the Hogwarts Boathouse!

A tip for Muggles visiting the wizarding world: Refresh your memory by re-reading Ms. Rowling's books and watching all of the films again because you are sure to notice so many more details in an around Diagon Alley and Hogsmeade!
Witch Wishes and Magically Yours,

Marianna Blackwater
Chief Witch, No-Maj Relations
The Magical Congress of the United States of America

*No-Maj is an American term meaning "No Magic" and is the American interchangeable term for Muggle, or people of no magic. For the purposes of this book, the more well known term, Muggle, is used.

INTRODUCTION

Welcome Muggles, Witches and Wizards to The Wizarding World of Harry Potter at Universal Orlando! Included in this informative volume is a wealth of information to navigate through one of America's most popular destinations, the enchanted land of Orlando, Florida.

Witches and Wizards as well as Muggles are welcomed to visit Universal Orlando, the home of magic sanctioned by the Minister for Magic in London. J. K. Rowling's stories about "the boy who lived" provide a perfect setting for Muggles to experience and make a little magic. These stories have brought such delight to Muggles, that many have taken to describing themselves as "Potter Geeks." Universal has created a wonderland to these Muggles to explore, taste, and even cast spells!

In the following chapters, follow Harry's steps and experience the wonder that Harry felt when he first stepped through the brick wall into Diagon Alley! Learn where to get Harry's favorite ice cream, purchase wands, and visit all aspects of Diagon Alley, the London Waterfront and Hogsmeade. Use this guide to navigate through the Wizarding World, but beware! Contained in this volume are many spoilers!

Throughout this volume, you will find Winks, magic hints to better your experience and to discover hidden gems placed for Muggle enjoyment and Wizard mirth. Also included throughout this volume are 25 Wizard Trivia Questions to test your level of Potter geekness!

Wink: Download the ebook version to your smart phone using the free Kindle App. You'll have expert Magic advice at your fingertips!

Wink: Yen Sid, the sorcerer in the Disney film, Fantasia, and his famous hat bear a striking resemblance to Dumbledore and his Sorting Hat, no?

"We are only as strong as we are united, as weak as we are divided."
Albus Dumbledore
Harry Potter and the Goblet of Fire

1 BUYING TICKETS FOR THE WIZARDING WORLD

The clever wizards at Universal Orlando, in an attempt to reduce any misuse of Muggle entertainment, cast many charms and enchantments on The Wizarding World of Harry Potter. Just as on the grounds of Hogwarts Castle in northern Scotland, wizards and witches are prevented from apparating and disapparating in the state of Florida. This being the case, Muggles, as well as wizards and witches, traveling to Orlando must purchase admission tickets to Hogsmeade and Diagon Alley and stay at one of the many inns (hotels) in Orlando. None of these hotels use wizard currency (Gold Galleons, Silver Sickles and Bronze Knuts) so stop by your local branch of Gringotts Bank to get muggle money (or what appears to be Muggle magic in the form of a "credit card" before traveling).

Tickets for Admission to the Wizarding World

Muggles and magical folk may purchase tickets at the entrance gates of Universal Orlando Resort. A more effective way, however, is to visit the Muggle website, www.universalorlando.com. In using this website, Muggles may save $20 American dollars on their tickets. However, if you wish to experience other parts of the resort, (there is a great deal of magic to be found in Marvel Super Hero Island, Seuss Landing and the Lost Continent at Islands of Adventure and there are many fantastic beasts to be found at Skull Island and at Men in Black in Universal Studios), you should purchase a multi-day ticket. These tickets come in different categories. No matter how many days you want to spend, be sure to choose the Park-to-Park option. This is the only way that you can travel back and forth between Hogsmeade and Diagon Alley on the Hogwarts Express train.

The current prices and ticket options are as follows (but subject to change by the crafty Universal Orlando wizards at any time):

Warning: Don't purchase passes from unknown vendors or online sites like Craigslist. While the passes might be valid, many travelers have been burned by purchasing these passes. Universal Orlando uses Muggle biometric technology. Upon using your ticket for the first time, you are required to scan your fingerprint. This eliminates sharing a pass with anyone. Many travelers have arrived at the gates and been denied entrance due to invalid passes. A safe discount site that has a good reputation is www.UndercoverTourist.com. This site also has a useful crowd calendar.

Types of Tickets

Tickets are available as One Day tickets or Multiple Day Tickets. When purchasing online, you may choose one of these options:

One Park Per Day tickets include access to either Universal Studios or Islands of Adventure for one day during park hours. Riding the Hogwarts Express train ride in The Wizarding World of Harry Potter is not included.

Park to Park tickets (similar to Disney's Park Hopper) allows unlimited access to two parks—Islands of Adventure and Universal Studios for one day during park hours. This type of ticket is required to ride the Hogwarts Express train ride in The Wizarding World of Harry Potter.

Two-Park Tickets include the two main theme parks—Universal Studios and Islands of Adventure.

Three-Park Tickets include the addition of Volcano Bay Waterpark.

Value Pricing One Day Tickets

> 1-Park, One Park Per Day Ticket:
> Adult $114, Child (ages 3-9): $109

> 2-Park, One Day Ticket:
> Adult $169, Child (ages 3-9): $164

Regular Pricing One Day Ticket

> 1-Park, One Park Per Day Ticket:
> Adult $122, Child (ages 3-9): $117

> 2-Park, One Day Ticket:
> Adult $177, Child (ages 3-9): $172

Anytime Pricing One Day Ticket

> 1-Park, One Park Per Day Ticket:
> Adult $129, Child: $124 (ages 3-9)

2-Park, One Day Ticket:
Adult $184, Child: $179

Ticket Combos

Combo tickets are available in two types. With multi-day tickets, you may choose between Two Park Ticket Combos and Three Park Ticket Combos. Two Park ticket combos include the two original parks, Universal Studios and Islands of Adventure. Three Park ticket combos include a day at Volcano Bay Water Park for an extra $55. Ticket combos are also available with the Park to Park option and the One Park Per Day option.

Two Park Tickets

2 Park Tickets include Admission to Universal Studios and/or Islands of Adventure.

2-Park, One Park Per Day Tickets

2 Day Admission: Adult $214.99, Child: $204.99 (ages 3-9)
3 Day Admission: Adult $234.99, Child: $224.99
4 Day Admission: Adult $244.99, Child: $234.99
5 Day Admission: Adult $254.99, Child: $244.99

2-Park, Park to Park Admission

This type of ticket is available for one day or multiple days. The more days you buy, the more you save. Park to Park access is required to ride the Hogwarts Express train ride which travels between the two main parks.

2 Day Admission: Adult: $274.99, Child $264.99
3 Day Admission: Adult: $294.99, Child $284.99
4 Day Admission: Adult: $304.99, Child $299.99
5 Day Admission: Adult: $324.99, Child $314.99

Three Park Tickets

Three park tickets include admission to Volcano Bay Water Park.

3-Park, One Park Per Day Tickets:

3-Day Admission: Adult: $244.99, Child: $234.99
4-Day Admission: Adult: $309.99, Child: $299.99
5-Day Admission: Adult: $324.99, Child: $314.99

3-Park, Park to Park Tickets:

2-Day Admission: Adult: $274.99, Child: $264.99
3-Day Admission: Adult: $294.99, Child: $284.99
4-Day Admission: Adult: $374.99, Child: $364.99
5-Day Admission: Adult: $389.99, Child: $399.99

Wink: If you visit more than once a year, the best value is an annual pass. See the section below.

Ticket Delivery Options

There are five options to receive your tickets.
Free ticket delivery options:

Mobile Ticket

This option is delivery by e-mail and to your account's Wallet. This is a useful option because you won't lose your tickets. However, keep your cell phone charged or you will not have use of your tickets.

Print at Home

With this option you'll have your tickets in advance. I never use this option because your printed paper tickets are difficult to manage and can be easily damaged in the rain or wet rides.

Will Call Kiosks

These are self service terminals which allow you to pick up your passes either the day before entering the parks early in the morning.

You may also pick up Will Call tickets at onsite hotel concierge desks. These are credit card sized tickets. I like this option when using a lanyard to keep your ticket, express pass, credit card and I. D. together. Be sure to have your confirmation number from your purchase for pickup.

There are two more delivery options with charges:

Ship to Home Domestic: $14. P. O. Box not available, allow five business days for processing and delivery. These will be paper card tickets.

Ship to Home International: $19. Allow 10-13 business days for processing and delivery. These will be paper card tickets.

Call Guest Services for more information at (407) 224-4233.

Annual Passes

If you will be visiting Universal Orlando for more four days or more, instead of buying Park to Park tickets, you may want to purchase an annual pass. The seasonal pass is the same price as a 4 day Park to Park pass, although there are black out dates.

Seasonal Annual Pass

2 Park Seasonal Pass: $304.99
3 Park Seasonal Pass: $403.99

The seasonal pass has black out dates included and does not include admission to special events such as Mardi Gras and concerts.

2019 Seasonal Pass Blockout Dates:

Universal Studios Florida™

2019 Blockout Dates:

> Jan. 1 - 3, 2019
> Apr. 12 - 27, 2019
> Jul. 1 - 31, 2019
> Dec. 21 - 31, 2019
> 2019 Concert dates*: Feb. 9, 16, 17, 23, Mar. 2, 9, 10, 16, 17, 23, 24, 30, 31

2020 Blockout Dates:

> Jan. 1 – 3, 2020
> Apr. 3 – 18, 2020
> Jul. 1 – 31, 2020
> Dec. 19 – 31, 2020

*Seasonal Passholders are blocked out of Universal Studios Florida™ on all concert dates and will only receive access to Universal's Islands of Adventure™. Additional concert dates will be announced at a later date and are subject to change.

Universal's Islands of Adventure™

2019 Blockout Dates:

> Jan. 1 - 3, 2019
> Apr. 12 - 27, 2019
> Jul. 1 - 31, 2019
> Dec. 21 - 31, 2019

2020 Blockout Dates:

Jan. 1 – 3, 2020
Apr. 3 – 18, 2020
Jul. 1 – 31, 2020
Dec. 19 – 31, 2020

Universal's Volcano Bay™

2019 Blockout Dates:

Apr. 12 – 27, 2019
Jun. 14 – Aug. 18, 2019

2020 Blockout Dates:

Apr. 3 – 18, 2020
Jun. 12 – Aug. 16, 2020

Note: Volcano Bay™ blockout dates apply to 3-Park Passes only.

Annual Power Pass

Power Pass benefits include 50% off parking in addition to discounts at hotels, special event tickets and Blue Man Group tickets. If you drive to Universal often or more than four days, it may be worth it to buy a Preferred Pass instead. The Power Pass has almost the same blackout dates as the Seasonal Pass. If you are not going to use a car, save money with the Seasonal Pass.

2 Park Power Pass: $354.99
3 Park Power Pass: $463.99

Power Pass Blockout Dates:

Universal Studios Florida™

2019 Blockout Dates:

    Jan. 1 - 3, 2019
    Apr. 12 - 27, 2019
    Dec. 21 - 31, 2019

2020 Blockout Dates:

    Jan. 1 – 3, 2020
    Apr. 3 – 18, 2020
    Dec. 19 – 31, 2020

Universal's Islands of Adventure™

2019 Blockout Dates:

    Jan. 1 - 3, 2019
    Apr. 12 - 27, 2019
    Dec. 21 - 31, 2019

2020 Blockout Dates:

    Jan. 1 – 3, 2020
    Apr. 3 – 18, 2020
    Dec. 19 – 31, 2020

Universal's Volcano Bay Blockout Dates

2019 Blockout Dates:
    Jun. 14 – Aug.18, 2019, before 4 pm.

2020 Blockout Dates:
    Jun. 12 – Aug. 16, 2020, before 4 pm.

Note: Volcano Bay™ blockout dates apply to 3-Park Passes only.

Annual Preferred Pass

The Preferred Pass is a good deal for guests who want to take advantage of the free parking benefit. If you take a car, this benefit will soon pay for itself after a few days.

2 Park Preferred Pass: $394.99
3 Park Preferred Pass: $503.99

There are no blockout dates at Universal Studios™ or at Universal's Island of Adventure™ for Preferred Annual Passholders. Preferred Passholders are blocked out on the following dates:

Universal's Volcano Bay Blockout Dates

2019 Blockout Dates:
Jul. 1 – Aug. 18, 2019, before 4pm

2020 Blockout Dates:
Jul. 1 – Aug. 16, 2020, before 4pm

Note: Volcano Bay™ blockout dates apply to 3-Park Passes only.

Annual Premier Pass

The Premier Pass is the highest priced pass because there are several advantages. The benefits associated with this level pay for the increase in price as long as you use them. This pass is great for Florida residents who will actually visit the parks several times a year. Only purchase this option if you will use the added benefits such as the Halloween Horror Nights ticket and discounts on dining. For many families, the best bet is for only one member to have this type of pass for the parking and discounts, and the rest of the family purchases a less expensive pass.

2 Park Premier Pass: $559.99
3 Park Premier Pass: $733.99

Exclusive Premier Pass Benefits:

- Universal Express after 4:00 pm

- Free Valet Parking (tipping is expected, excludes holidays and special events)

- Free self parking

- Early Park Admission to the Wizarding World of Harry Potter

- 15% off on multi-day theme park admission tickets purchased at the front gate (Up to 6 people per transaction per day; not valid on tickets including Wet 'n Wild® admission, or Universal Express™ passes, or tickets with Universal Express™)

- One (1) free Halloween Horror Nights ticket* (select nights)

- 15% off all restaurants (excluding food & beverage carts and alcoholic beverages)

- 15% off at Universal Orlando™ select merchandise stores and carts (restrictions apply on select merchandise)

- All club access to CityWalk™ for Passholders (excludes concerts and special events)

- Save up to 30%1 off room rates at each Premier and Preferred on-site hotel or save up to 25%1 off room rates at Universal's Cabana Bay Beach Resort

- One (1) free Halloween Horror Nights ticket* (select nights)

- 15% off at select restaurants (excluding food & beverage carts and alcoholic beverages)

- 15% off at Universal Orlando™ owned and operated merchandise stores and carts (restrictions apply on select merchandise)

- All club access to CityWalk™ for Passholders (excludes concerts and special events)

- Save up to 30% off room rates at onsite hotels

- Free admission to select special events such as Mardi Gras and Grinchmas™

Visit UniversalOrlando.com for more information.

Wink: Buy only one Preferred Pass! Only one member of your party needs this pass to get the parking benefit or other discounts. Save by purchasing less expensive passes for the rest of your family.

The Wizarding World of Harry Potter™ Exclusive Vacation Package

Muggles and wizards alike can experience all the magic and excitement of the Wizarding World with an exclusive Harry Potter vacation package! It includes various benefits such as Park to Park theme park admissions, hotel accommodations and Early Park Admission (with paid theme park admission) to The Wizarding World of Harry Potter one hour before the theme parks open. Plus, you'll get breakfast at Three Broomsticks™, Leaky Cauldron™ and more.

This vacation package starts from $109 per person, per night, based on a family of four. The price depends on availability, time of year and hotel selection. Air travel can also be booked through the website. The hotels available are both onsite and offsite hotels with less expensive pricing for staying offsite.

This exclusive vacation package includes:

• 5-Night Hotel Accommodations

• 3-Park 2-Day Park-to-Park Ticket with 2 Days Free1 to Universal Studios Florida™, Universal's Islands of Adventure™ AND Universal's Volcano Bay™ (Valid for bookings now – 3/14/19 and travel now – 5/31/19 (Blockout Dates Apply)

• Breakfast at the Leaky Cauldron™ in Universal Studios Florida™—one per person

• Breakfast at the Three Broomsticks™ in Universal's Islands of Adventure™—one per person

• Early Park Admission to The Wizarding World of Harry Potter™ and Universal's Volcano Bay™ one hour before the park opens (valid theme park admission required).

• One Shutterbutton's™ Photography Studio session in The Wizarding World of Harry Potter™ – Diagon Alley™

• Access to select live entertainment venues at Universal CityWalk™

For Package Arrivals after May 31, 2019:

• Package will include a 3-Park 4-Day Park-to-Park Ticket which includes admission to Universal Studios Florida™, Universal's Islands of Adventure AND Universal's Volcano Bay™

Call To Book: (877) 801-9720

Military Tickets and Packages

Universal Orlando offers specially priced tickets to Leisure Travel offices at U. S. military bases for re-sale to active duty, retired military and Department of Defense personnel. Ticket pricing is determined by the local Leisure Travel offices. Active duty military with valid military IDs can receive a discount when purchasing multi-day tickets at the front gate tickets windows at Universal Orlando Resort.™

A special Military vacation package is also available.
Military Vacation Package Includes:

- 3-Night Hotel Accommodations
- 3-Park 4-Day Park-to-Park Military Promotional Ticket 1 to Universal Studios Florida™, Universal's Islands of Adventure™ AND
- Universal's Volcano Bay™
- Early Park Admission 2 to The Wizarding World of Harry Potter™ and Universal's Volcano Bay™ one hour before the park opens (valid theme park admission required, select attractions).
- Access to select live entertainment venues1 at Universal CityWalk™

To book your vacation, call 1-888-340-4614 or visit your military base ticket office (ITT/LTS).

Visit the following links for more information.

Military Vacation Packages:
http://www.visitorlando.com/discounts-and-tickets/militarydiscounts

http://www.shadesofgreen.org/UniversalOrlando.htm

"It is our choices, Harry, that show what we truly are, far more than our abilities."
Albus Dumbledore
Harry Potter and the Chamber of Secrets

2 WHERE WIZARDS CAN REST LIKE MUGGLES

The Universal Orlando wizards have divulged many wizarding secrets, but letting Muggles spend nights in the wizarding world is going a bit too far. The Ministry of Magic has decreed that some secrets must be kept. There are no guest rooms in either The Leaky Cauldron or in the Village of Hogsmeade for Muggles at Universal Orlando.

Onsite Resorts

Touring the Wizarding World of Harry Potter is quite an exhausting experience since broomstick travel and apparating is strictly forbidden. After a long day, what could be better than to relax at a resort right on the property?

Magical and non-magical guests have their choice when it comes to lodging in Orlando. If you are going to spend the majority of your time in Florida at the Wizarding World of Harry Potter, then perhaps the best choice is a Universal Orlando onsite hotel. There are six onsite hotels from which to choose and each has its own special qualities. Three of the original hotels offer "Universal Express," a fantastic feature which lets you into the short line on many rides as well as top notch accommodations. The greatest advantage to staying at any onsite hotel is that you are granted Early Park Admission to the Wizarding World of Harry Potter. Early Park Admission grants admission one hour before the general population of Muggles are admitted. All onsite hotels are run by the Loews family of hotels, quite an enterprising group of Muggles who are known for their dedication to quality lodging. A seventh value hotel complex is currently under construction.

There are several categories for onsite hotels and are listed here.

Premier Resorts

The three original onsite hotels are the finest accommodations at Universal Orlando. These hotels offer special benefits to their guests.

Loews Portofino Bay Resort

In what seems a feat of magic, the Loews team of Muggles have brought the Italian Riviera to Orlando at the Loews Portofino Bay Resort. This "seaside" resort is the most luxurious and well equipped hotel at Universal Orlando. It is comprised of 750 guest rooms, 45 suites, 7 restaurants, a spa, concierge floor, fitness room, and three swimming pools. The hotel offers something special for little ones and families—the

Despicable Me Suites. These are two bedroom suites with a Minion theme in the children's bedroom. There is a king sized bed in the parents room and two full sized bed in the kids room. The room is advertised to only accommodate 5 guests.

Hard Rock Hotel

American Muggles love their rock 'n roll stars and at the Hard Rock Hotel, you'll be treated like a muggle rock star. The property has 650 guest rooms, including 29 suites, and a 12,000 square foot pool with Muggle entertainments such as a water slide, sandpit for children and another feat of Muggle ingenuity, under-water speakers playing rock music. The resort has a pool bar and grill as well as hotel bar and restaurants, both casual and fine dining.

Loews Royal Pacific Resort

For anyone who has visited the South Seas, they will recognize the lush landscape, exotic palms and sandy beach at the Loews Royal Pacific Resort. The magic here is in enjoying a South Seas vacation without sailing halfway around the globe. The property has 1,000 guest rooms including 51 suites and a lagoon style pool. Conde Nast Traveler gave it their Readers' Choice Award in the "Top 150 Resorts in Mainland U.S." for two years in a row. The hotel also received the top slot in Travel + Leisure magazine's "Top 50—Best Family Resorts in the U. S. and Canada" list more than once. Dine in at one of the fantastic restaurants including a sushi bar, American grill and a luau dinner show. Staying at this resort will definitely allow magical folk to experience luxury as they are rich Muggles.

Premier Resort Benefits:

• Free Universal Express — Unlimited ride access to skip the regular lines in both theme parks (not available on the two most popular Harry Potter rides).

- Early park admission to the Wizarding World of Harry Potter one hour before the theme park opens (valid theme park admission required).

- Complimentary water taxis and shuttle buses to both theme parks and CityWalk.

- Priority seating at select restaurants throughout both theme parks and CityWalk.

- Access to pool areas at all onsite resorts

- Merchandise purchased at the parks or CityWalk delivered to your room

- Free WiFi

- Discounts at select restaurants and shops at CityWalk and the parks

In addition to these benefits, each deluxe hotel offers Club Level rooms with these additional benefits:

- Evening turndown service, and cotton signature bathrobes

- Access to a private lounge

- Personal concierge services to help with all your vacation needs

- Complimentary coffee, assorted teas, and soft drinks throughout the day

- Continental breakfast served each morning

- Hot & cold hors d'oeuvres and complimentary beer and wine

- Dessert treats each night

Preferred Resort

Loews Sapphire Falls Resort

The Caribbean themed Loews Sapphire Falls Resort is located between Royal Pacific and Cabana Bay Beach Resort. The Muggle "magic" transports guests to a paradise where blue waterfalls cascade into sparkling pools.

The resort is a tropical jewel with a luxuriously landscaped 16,000 square foot pool surrounded by waterfalls. "Ruins" of a stone turret are the centerpiece of the modern-chic lobby. The 1,000 guest rooms and suites are designed with a focus on comfort. The resort's design is based on old-world timelessness while still being chic and modern.

Dining options include a full-service restaurant with a view of the water, a poolside bar and grill, a rum bar and a casual Caribbean-style market. The hotel will also offers a fitness center with a dry sauna, a white sand beach, a water slide, a children's play area, and cabana rentals. This moderately priced resort gives guests the feel of a luxury resort.

Prime Value Resorts

Loews Cabana Bay Beach Resort

Because not all Wizards and Muggles are as rich as the Malfoy's, a more economical hotel option is also available onsite but with lots of amenities. Loews Cabana Bay Beach Resort features a fun retro theme that takes you back to the iconic beach resorts of the 1950's and 60's. Just because it is less expensive, doesn't mean that there aren't numerous amenities to enjoy. Guest staying here enjoy two giant swimming pools with a waterslide, lazy river, 10-lane bowling alley, and Early Park Admission to The Wizarding World of Harry Potter one hour before the theme parks open. When bringing the whole Muggle family, you might choose to stay in a family suite that sleeps six, complete with a kitchenette, or a two bedroom suite. The hotel is within walking distance of Universal CityWalk dining and entertainment complex, and the Wizarding World or guests can take one of the complimentary shuttle buses that whisk guests back and forth (broomsticks are strictly prohibited). Dining options include a food court which stays open late, Galaxy Bowl Restaurant in the hotel's bowling alley, poolside dining and a hotel bar. Coffee and tea are available at Starbucks® in the lobby.

Universal's Aventura Hotel

The most recent addition to the group of onsite hotels is The Aventura Hotel. It is a very modern glass high rise structure will reflect light while the rooms will project serenity. The rooms are also very modern with a tablet which controls the lights and television (Wizards have a bit of trouble with these features). There is an open air rooftop restaurant and bar and fantastic food options including Starbuck in the lobby.

Value Resorts

A new resort hotel complex is currently under construction. Universal's Endless Summer Resort with have two hotels. The first hotel will open during the summer in 2019. The Surfside Inn and Suites is located nearby Universal Orlando on the site of the old Wet 'n Wild Waterpark on International Drive.

When this hotel complex opens, it will be the least expensive onsite resort option. These two hotels are the only hotels which are not walking distance to the theme park. Shuttle buses will take guests back and forth to the hotel. Rooms are advertised as low as $73 per night plus tax based on a 7-night stay.

"If you want to know what a man's like, take a good look at how he treats his inferiors, not his equals."
Sirius Black
Harry Potter and the Goblet of Fire

3 THE LONDON WATERFRONT

More than just a facade to hide Diagon Alley, the London Waterfront at Universal Studios Florida brings famous London landmarks to the Wizarding World of Harry Potter. If it weren't for the steamy heat of the Florida climate, you might believe you've been transported to London. The photographic opportunities abound is this small gateway area between San Francisco and World Expo. Many a hapless Muggle walks right past, not realizing the wizardry of Diagon Alley taking place just beyond. If you'd like to experience magic as Harry did, this should be your first stop on your way to Diagon Alley. Mind you, most Muggles miss details on their first trip. There's so much to take in, so take your time. The best advice is to arrive very early when most Muggles are still in bed. Early Park

Admission is a wonderful benefit for onsite hotel guests because it gets very crowded each day no matter the time of year. However, since many Muggles rush through this area, you should visit it at any time of day.

Kings Cross Station

Flanking the left side of the London Waterfront is Kings Cross Station. While it may seem to some to be just the queue for the Hogwarts Express, Kings Cross is more. Musical performers called "street buskers" are very often stationed at the entrance. As you enter, relish the air conditioning which completes the London feel of the place. Take your time walking through the station and notice the advertisements. You'll find a large advertisement that is remarkably similar to one in front of which Dumbledore appeared to Harry in the film, Harry Potter and the Half Blood Prince. The "magic" of walking through to Platform 9 3/4 is so subtle, that you might not notice it happening.

Wink: Have someone film you crossing "through" the brick wall from behind.

Wink: Hermione's voice sounds distinctly different during the Hogwarts Express ride. It's not clear whether this is the work of a dark wizard or just a prank by one of the Weasley brothers.

Charing Cross Road

Charing Cross Road is a short stretch of road next to Kings Cross Station and is part of the waterfront area containing shopfronts, a park and the Leaky Cauldron. Most muggles do not even notice the Leaky Cauldron sign. As written in Harry Potter and the Philosopher's Stone, by J. K. Rowling:

"It was a tiny, grubby-looking pub. If Hagrid hadn't pointed it out, Harry wouldn't have noticed it was there. The people hurrying by didn't glance at it. Their eyes slid from the big book shop on one side to the record shop on the other as if they couldn't see the Leaky Cauldron at all."

The door to this "pub" is located between Screed and Sons Book Shop and a record shop but no matter how many times you cast "Alohomora," the door will not open. Browse the shop windows for winks. To the right is Leicester Station which is the nearest hidden entrance to Diagon Alley. Also with entrances to Diagon Alley is the famous Wyndham Theater. Across the lane is a park with the Eros Fountain from Piccadilly Circus.

The Knight Bus

Next to the Eros Fountain is the Knight Bus. This is a mode of wizard travel (other modes include broomsticks, apparition, and the Floo Network, all of which are banned from Universal Orlando) which takes travelers to all destinations— but nothing underwater. A conductor is there to greet you as well as the talking shrunken head. Have a little chat with him and maybe he will let you peek inside the bus.

Wizard Trivia Question #1: What name did Harry give the Knight bus conductor when asked for his name?

No. 12 Grimmauld Place

Grimmauld Place, a residential lane, is located in the London Borough of Islington. On this lane is No. 12 Grimmauld Place, the ancestral home of the Black family, famous for dark magic.

Harry Potter is the current owner having inherited it from his Godfather, Sirius Black. The bricks are darkened on this house because of all of the dark magic which has taken place. Look up to the second floor window to occasionally see Kreacher, the Black family house elf, peeking out at all of the nosy Muggles.

Across the lane from Grimmauld place is a London Taxi Hut. In London, these were originally the first drive-through food stops for hackney cab drivers. Light British meals such as jacket potatoes (known as loaded baked potatoes to American Muggles), sodas and snacks are sold here. Across from the record shop is another London Taxi Hut selling British Muggle merchandise which is not sold anywhere else in the parks.

A last British landmark is very popular for photographs. The red telephone booth is a very popular with Muggles crowding in for photos.

Wink: A faulty charm was placed on the telephone dial in the red phone booth to connect you to the Ministry of Magic by dialing M-A-G-I-C.

Hogwarts Express London

Like the one in the films, this unique train is one of a kind. It is the first "ride" from inside a theme park to bring riders into a different theme park. The London Hogwarts Express takes riders to Hogsmeade Station in Islands of Adventure. After crossing through to Platform 9 3/4, make your way around the luggage carts carrying Hogwarts students trunks and owls.

Step into your role as a Hogwarts student and experience the wonder Harry felt in a comfortable compartment with air conditioning, cushioned seats and large "window" out of which to see the passing sights of London and the journey to Hogwarts. Alas, you cannot buy something from the cart, but you can purchase a snack or beverage from the snack bar in the station and take it with you.

A few characters from the books are heard and seen during the train ride including Rubeus Hagrid, played by Robbie Coltrane. Notice the menacing Malfoy Manor on the way and try not to be frightened by Dementors! These chilling aspects are so brief, that all ages can ride easily.

Do not despair if you have a wheelchair or electronic conveyance vehicle (ECV). The Hogwarts Prefects will assist you and put your vehicle on the train for you and have it waiting for you in Hogsmeade. Rented strollers must be turned in at the station and a new one issued at the next station.

"It takes a great deal of bravery to stand up to our enemies, but just as much to stand up to our friends."
Albus Dumbledore
Harry Potter and the Sorcerer's Stone

4 DIAGON ALLEY

Wizardry abounds as you step through the opening in the bricks and take in the wondrous first sight of Diagon Alley. In this unique land, magic is made daily by Muggles, Witches and Wizards. Muggles have their first ever opportunity to cast spells with interactive wands. You can exchange Muggle money for Wizard currency and get a taste of wizards' brews available nowhere else in the world.

Muggles staying at an onsite hotels are allowed to arrive early every day for their chance to cast a little magic and experience the sights and sounds of the Wizarding World of Harry Potter. Plan to spend a significant part of your day in

Diagon Alley because there is so much to see and experience. After numerous visits, guests are still finding there is more to discover.

Diagon Alley is actually comprised of four "streets." Of course, there is Diagon Alley; turn right onto Horizont Alley and proceed to Carkitt Market. The entrance to Knockturn Alley is just past The Leaky Cauldron. With the exception of Knockturn Alley, the three streets form a triangle.

How to Find Diagon Alley

The clever Universal Studios wizards have done such a good job of disguising the entrance, that many a Muggle walks past without any idea of the magic just beyond. Enter Universal Studios through the giant arch, let the Muggle attendants scan your ticket and walk straight ahead through Production Central to the New York Area.

Turn right at Macy's and head through San Francisco until King's Cross Station is in sight. Pass the book shop and record shop and enter through Leicester Station. Follow the path to the brick opening and take a moment to savor your first glimpse of the immersive wizarding world. The Leaky Cauldron is on the left. Many a Muggle has been reduced to tears at the majestic sight of Diagon Alley!

Wink: Examine the interesting fountain in the brick wall at the entrance. It depicts a goblin statue crafted into a fountain. Why is it in the wall? Perhaps he was disgraced. One can only imagine that his likeness was bricked over when disguising Diagon Alley from Muggles.

Touring the Alley Street by Street

The streets or lanes of Diagon Alley are laid out in a "triangle," but there are actually four lanes. They are listed here as follows:

Diagon Alley
Knockturn Alley
Horizont Alley
Carkitt Market

Diagon Alley Attractions

On Diagon Alley, you'll find several establishments open for business, offering meals, wares and beverages. There are also many businesses with sealed entrances. These establishments have proprietors uncomfortable with conducting business with Muggles. Here are businesses which are open to Muggles for the selling of wares or refreshments including a couple of new businesses.

The Leaky Cauldron

Hagrid's favorite pub, The Leaky Cauldron, is open to Muggles from all over the world. Breakfast, lunch and dinner are served at this fine establishment and popular standards of British pub fare are available on the menu as well as a Kids Menu and Desserts. For more information, see Chapter 9: Fantastic Eats and Where to Find Them.

Madam Malkin's Robes for all Occasions

Wizard robes, Hogwarts House sweaters, scarves, gloves, sweatshirts, backpacks and accessories in all house colors are available for sale in this shop. Notice the Mirror of Erised, and mannequins featuring dress robes worn by Celestina Warbeck, Kingsley Shacklebolt, Dumbledore and Hermione's Yule Ball gown. While there, you should have the experience of being fitted for your Hogwarts house robes.

Wizard Trivia Question #2: Who did Harry meet for the first time at Madam Malkin's when he got measured for his wizard robes?

Shutterbutton's Photography Studio

One form of magic that Muggles are entranced by is moving wizard photography. At Shutterbutton's, Muggles can create a DVD photo album featuring themselves in different scenes from the Wizarding World. A wizard or witch team member will usher you into small green screen room with a vintage steampunk style camera mounted to the wall. You will then be given suggestions as to how to behave in each scene while being photographed. When completed, the team member will show you three preview scenes and offer the DVD for purchase to see the rest. The DVD comes in two cases, soft plastic for about $70 or metal case for about $80. A Shutterbuttons photo session is included in the Harry Potter Vacation Package. Shutterbuttons photo sessions are not included in My Universal Photos packages.

Quality Quidditch Supplies

It's not hard to find Ron Weasley's favorite shop. It's across the lane from the Leaky Cauldron and next to Weasley's Wizard Wheezes. Quidditch jerseys, broomsticks, bludger sets, golden snitches and all types of Ravenclaw, Hufflepuff, Slytherin and Gryffindor practice uniforms and jerseys can be purchased here. This store also carries t-shirts flaunting the emblems of your favorite international Quidditch teams.

Weasley's Wizard Wheezes

Giggles abound in this whimsical shop founded by Fred and George Weasley. Its storefront is one of the icons of the area with George's top hat lifting to reveal a magic rabbit. It is one of the first sights to encounter when entering Diagon Alley.

The interior is a feast for the eyes with many whimsical items for sale such as Extendable Ears, U No Poo, Puking Pastilles, and Sneak-o-scopes. Look up to see Weasley magical fireworks and Delores Umbridge tightroping on a unicycle. While it looks like a two or three story shop, only the first floor is accessible to Muggles.

Best souvenir items at Weasley's:

> Extendable Ears
> Cycling Dolores Umbridge
> Pygmy Puffs
> Screaming Yo Yo
> Boxing Telescope

Best edibles at Weasley's:

> Fever Fudge
> U No Poo
> Puking Pastilles
> Fainting Fancies
> Nosebleed Nougat

Wizard Trivia Question #3: What pet did Jenny choose from her brothers' shop to take to Hogwarts?

Ollivanders

No visit to Diagon Alley is complete without a visit to Ollivanders to see "The Wand Chooses the Wizard" ceremony. During each visit to Ollivanders, one visitor will be chosen to test a wand with a few spells and have a wand choose them. After the ceremony, exit through Ollivanders Wand Shop where you can choose your favorite wand which might be a replica of one that belonged to one of your favorite characters. Notice details around the shop like the Celtic Tree Calendar on the wall. Ollivanders has absolutely the best personal service in Diagon Alley.

Wink: Should your wand get broken, bring it back to Ollivanders and they will take it in the back to "magically" fix it.

Florean Fortescue's Ice Cream Parlour

As the Florida heat intensifies, a stop in at Harry's favorite ice cream parlour is exactly what the doctor ordered. Florean's offers a deliciously unique array of flavours in soft serve and hand packed ice creams. The showpiece flavour is Butterbeer Ice Cream. Other popular flavours include Chocolate Chili, Earl Grey and Lavender, Sticky Toffee Pudding and Harry's favorite, Strawberry Peanut Butter. Sundaes can be purchased in a souvenir glass.

Knockturn Alley Attractions

A visit to Diagon Alley would not be complete for some without a venture into this dark arts marketplace. Barely visible to Muggles (and Hufflepuffs for that matter), Knockturn Alley is just beyond The Leaky Cauldron. Notice the chill in the air as your eyes adjust to the darkness when you enter this lane. The chill in the air is a wonderful escape from the high heat of Florida. Knockturn Alley has lots of opportunities to cast some of the most imaginative spells in the area. The sky in this area is enchanted like the great hall in Hogwarts Castle, except that it is perpetually night here.

Borgin and Burkes

The only shop open to Muggles in Knockturn Alley is an attraction and a shop combined. Skulls, Death Eater masks, sinister items and clothing are available for purchase. The cursed necklace meant for Dumbledore is in a glass case, among other secrets to be found as well as t-shirts with wanted posters for Bellatrix Lestrange and Sirius Black.

Wizard Trivia Question #4: When Harry accidentally arrived in Borgin and Burkes by way of the Floo Network, in what did Harry hide so that the Malfoy's would not see him?

Horizont Alley Attractions

Horizont Alley is a very short lane but with the distinction of being home to Gringotts Wizarding Bank. The iconic bank building is home to both Harry Potter and the Escape from Gringotts attraction and Wiseacre's Wizarding Equipment, a shop from which Gringotts riders exit.

Harry Potter and the Escape from Gringotts

Goblins and wizards have collaborated to bring to Diagon Alley its feature attraction. Universal Studios' Wizards kept the Muggle public (who were already entranced by the magic in the Village of Hogsmeade) waiting without many clues as to what kind of ride this would be. As it turns out, it is two attractions in one with an elegant and extensive queue which takes Muggle guests through the great lobby of Gringotts Wizarding Bank.

Upon starting your tour, the very strict Gringotts security guards will direct you through the grand lobby with its crystal chandeliers, marble columns and gold gilt ornate finishes. You may speak to the busy goblins at work, but be prepared to be stared down by these unfriendly clerks. These goblins are in fact a product of Muggle "magic" better known as audio animatronic engineering. The head Goblin, Bogrod, who sits upon the raised podium gives instructions on how to enter a vault.

The queue then takes guests through the office hallway, passing a number goblin offices to Bill Weasley's office (all the while being monitored by guards). From there you enter the lift in which riders descend miles down into the cavernous underground depths to access vault carts. At the cart loading station, riders load four across in the carts. Four connected carts launch on the journey through the caverns of Gringotts depths.

The journey starts out on a metal roller coaster track, but this is no ordinary roller coaster ride. Be prepared for a multi-dimensional experience. You will go backwards, have sudden stops, high speed chases and spinning. On this multi-dimensional ride, you'll encounter troll guards, a couple of dark wizards including "He who must not be named," a dragon and even our favorite trio, Harry, Ron and Hermione.

The cast of Harry Potter and the Escape from Gringotts includes several actors reprising their roles for the films:

Helena Bonham Carter as Bellatrix Lestrange
Ralph Fiennes as Lord Voldemort
Domhnall Gleeson as Bill Weasley
Rupert Grint as Ron Weasley
Daniel Radcliffe as Harry Potter
Emma Watson, Hermione Granger

Riders must be 42 inches tall, and all loose articles and bags must be stowed in the temporary lockers on the outside of Gringotts Wizarding Bank. A single-rider line is usually available for this attraction. This ride is less scary than the original Harry Potter ride in Hogsmeade.

Tip: Take the opportunity to ride this in the morning or late afternoon when the wait times are shorter.

Wink: Riding in the last row of the cart is a little more thrilling than in the first row.

Globus Mundi

The newest shop in Diagon Alley is a Wizarding World Travel Agency for wizards and witches. The walls are covered with posters of places where wizards wish to travel. There is a variety of merchandise at this fine establishment for sale including Hogwarts Express shirts and merchandise and Globus Mundi Coffee Tumblers.

The Fountain of Fair Fortune

Named after the famous story from The Tales of Beedle the Bard, this is a nice little pub to get a beverage. Try a Butterbeer, either chilled and topped with cream or frozen, a refreshing Fishy Green Ale or an ale brew exclusive to Diagon Alley such as the Wizards' Brew or Dragon Scale.

Magical Menagerie

This is the shop from which Hogwarts students buy their magical pets. Available for purchase are feathery snowy white owls, phoenix, scaly creatures and furry friends. Look up to see Luna's favorite beast, the triple horned Snorkak.

Wink: Speak to the huge python in the window to find out if you speak Parcel Tongue!

Wiseacre's Wizarding Equipment

As you exit Escape from Gringotts, stop to browse this interesting shop. If you are looking for Hogwarts Express shirts and merchandise, this is the shop. Find all sorts of Wizarding World of Harry Potter merchandise including t-shirts, magnifying glasses, crystal balls, telescopes and more.

Scribbulus

At Scribbulus, a Hogwarts student or a visiting Muggle can find stationary, assorted feather quills, backpacks, journals with Hogwarts house insignias, lanyards and even howlers!

Carkitt Market Area Attractions

The Carkitt Market area resembles some of London's quaint markets, however there is more to do than just shop. Here is what you may find in side Carkitt Market:

Gringotts Money Exchange

In this small office next to Harry Potter and the Escape from Gringotts, Muggles may direct questions to the attending goblin and exchange their Muggle currency for wizard money to keep as souvenirs or spend in the theme parks. This is one of the few "character" experiences in the wizarding world.

Eternelle's Elixir of Refreshment

At this kiosk, Gilly Water is sold along with a choice of four different flavoured elixirs to quench the thirst.

The Hopping Pot

This is a walk-up pub style bar with picnic tables and counter service with most of the same menu as the Leaky Cauldron. The tables offer a great view of the alternating shows performed in Carkitt Market.

Mermaid Statue

One of the most popular spell casting spots is the Mermaid Statue, inspired from the film, Harry Potter and the Goblet of Fire. Many an unsuspecting Muggle gets wet from this spewing fountain!

Celestina Warbeck and the Banshees

At Diagon Alley, everyone can enjoy the jazzy, musical stylings from the "singing sorceress," Celestina Warbeck, the long time favorite of Mrs. Weasley. Along with the Banshees, Ms. Warbeck entertains and occasionally calls a Muggle up to perform with her!

The Tales of Beedle the Bard

Yet another Confundus Curse must have been placed when J. K. Rowling was allowed to publish The Tales of Beedle the Bard in book form. These tales became famous with Muggles in the film, Harry Potter and the Deathly Hallows, Part One. In Carkitt Market, elaborate puppet shows of the two most famous tales entertain Muggles each day at alternating times. Performance times vary, but The Tale of the Three Brother's and The Fountain of Fair Fortune puppet shows are performed every 45 minutes or so.

Wands by Gregorvitch

Dumbledore's Slytherin House contemporary, Mykew Gregorovitch's wand shop is managed at Diagon Alley by mysterious wizards who remain from sight.
In this legendary wand maker's shop, a wide assortment of character wands replicas are available for purchase. This stand is much favored by Muggles in a hurry and not looking for the level of service offered at Ollivanders.

Wink: Gregorovitch wands are favored by students from the House of Slytherin.

Owl Post

Another new addition to Diagon Alley is a Shipping Service. At Owl Post, Muggles can have their purchases boxed

and shipped in packaging just like those which are delivered by owls to Hogwarts students. Packages are shipped anywhere in the continental United States.

Sugarplum's Sweet Shop

At Sugarplum's Muggles can satisfy their sweet tooth with the sweet confections of the wizarding world. Every nook is stocked with colourful sweets and tasty temptations sure to satisfy even the most traditional Muggles. Choose from Exploding Bon Bons, Acid Pops, Pepper Imps, Pink Coconut Ice or my favorite, Peppermint Chocolate Toads. Found in the glass case are baked treats like Cauldron Cakes, Pumpkin Pasties and Butterbeer Fudge.

"I hope you're pleased with yourselves. We could all have been killed — or worse, expelled."
Hermione Granger
Harry Potter and the Sorcerer's Stone

5 THE VILLAGE OF HOGSMEADE

In 2010, wizards changed a struggling theme park into a worldwide destination thanks to the opening of The Wizarding World of Harry Potter—Hogsmeade at Universal's Islands of Adventure. With Universal Orlando's attention to detail and J. K. Rowling's creative control, this new "land" continues to draw visitors who want to visit Hogwarts Castle. In Islands of Adventure, you can mail a post card with a Hogsmeade postmark. After all of these years, guests are still discovering new details about this enchanted destination.

Harry Potter and the Forbidden Journey

The centerpiece of Hogsmeade is the iconic Hogwarts Castle which can be seen from miles away. The castle is home to two attractions in one. Guests may take a walk-through "castle tour" which is a tour through the queue of the attraction, Harry Potter and the Forbidden Journey. The second part of the attraction is a four minute multi-sensory, multi-dimensional ride which uses ground breaking Kuka-Arm technology which tips you backwards, forwards and swings in all directions. This award winning ride gives you the sensation of flying on "benches."

The Castle Tour

For Muggles who do not wish to board the ride, the Castle Tour is the best way to discover and enjoy the secrets of Hogwarts. The tour begins with you joining a group of Muggles to attend a lecture on the history of Hogwarts Castle. Follow the tour by entering at the Dungeons. On your right is the statue of the hump-backed witch marking the entrance to the underground tunnel into Honeydukes. On your left, you will notice the Mirror of Erised and the Potions Classroom door. As you continue on, you will pass through the greenhouses where Hogwarts students study Herbology.

The queue leads back into the castle through a corridor with a gold statue of the architect of Hogwarts Castle. Located next to the statue are the four jewel hour glasses which mark the progress for the Hogwarts House Cup (Gryffindor is in the lead, of course). The next statue is the first headmaster of Hogwarts and then we see the gold Gryphon statue which marks the entrance to Professor Dumbledore's office.

As the tour continues, we come to a favorite place of mine, the portrait gallery. Among others, the four founders of Hogwarts are pictured and are having a heated discussion concerning Muggles in the Castle. Of course, Salazar Slytherin is disturbed by the onlooking Muggles.

Wink: Look for the founders' personal items in the talking portraits, some of which will become Voldemort's horcruxes.

We pass through to Dumbledore's office and meet the great wizard, himself as he warns of a dragon on the loose. Next, as we enter the dark arts classroom (go slowly through this room because there is so much to see), we are interrupted by Harry, Ron and Hermione who invite you to a Quidditch match!

We are directed to the Gryffindor Common Room where we meet The Fat Lady's portrait, who guards the entrance and isn't happy about letting in Muggles into the Gryffindor Common Room without a password! Down the hall is the Sorting Hat giving instructions on boarding the ride once you reach the Room of Requirement. As the Sorting Hat says, "You must be more than Goblin size, at least 48 inches tall to ride." The Sorting Hat is located in the "Room of Requirement." This is just beyond the Gryffindor Common Room and it is basically the end of the Castle Tour. There are videos showing the ride vehicles so that you know a little of what to expect on the ride.

Wink: The statue of the hump-backed witch at the castle entrance is first seen in the film, Harry Potter and the Sorcerer's Stone, in the scene just before Ron, Harry, and Hermione find Hagrid's three headed dog, Fluffy.

The Forbidden Journey

As you enter the room of requirement you are entering the loading platform for the ride. This is a moving platform which means the ride vehicles are in constant motion. This moving platform moves quite quickly. The attendants can direct you to a stationary platform if you need assistance boarding. There is a place to enter the ride vehicle on a stationary platform.

The attendant will secure a shoulder harness in place on your enchanted bench before the ride begins. There are no loops on this ride, but it does tip you backwards and almost upside down at one point. Muggle feet will dangle on this ride so appropriate footwear should be worn. Many a Muggle has lost a flip flop sandal on the ride.

The journey begins as Hermione casts a spell and enchants the bench which sends guests through the Floo Network. We are then met by Harry and Ron on broomsticks and we are off to a Quidditch Match. Things don't go as planned as you encounter an escaped dragon. We are chased into the Forbidden Forest where you encounter scary things such as giant spiders and the Whomping Willow.

Eventually you head back to the Quidditch Pitch where you are chased by Dementors into the Chamber of Secrets. There you'll encounter the terrifying Basilisk and more Dementors. Harry casts the Expecto Patronum spell just as you are about to receive the Dementor's Kiss and then it is back to celebrate Gryffindor's victory! Dumbledore sends you traveling back through the Floo Network to exit the ride. The filmed sequences in Harry Potter and the Forbidden Journey features many actors who were cast as the same characters of the film series including:

Daniel Radcliffe as Harry Potter
Emma Watson as Hermione Granger
Rupert Grint as Ron Weasley
Michael Gambon as Albus Dumbledore
Robbie Coltrane as Rubeus Hagrid
Tom Felton as Draco Malfoy
Mathew Lewis as Neville Longbottom
Bonnie Wright as Ginny Weasley
James Phelps as Fred Weasley
Oliver Phelps as George Weasley
Warwick Davis as Professor Flitwick

Guests are not permitted to bring any bags or loose items on this attraction. Free temporary lockers are available on your right as you enter the dungeons, but using one of these lockers can be a scene of chaos on a busy day. The best idea is to rent an all day locker to store valuables. If worried about fitting into the "enchanted benches" there is a bench outside the entrance to sit in to try it out for size. As you exit the ride, pick up your belongings from the lockers and then wander through Filch's Emporium of Confiscated Goods.

Some guests who have ridden this ride have had serious reactions. Those prone to motion sickness or Vertigo are to ride with caution or not ride.

Wink: Look for a broken Enchanted Bench under the Whomping Willow!

Filch's Emporium of Confiscated Goods

As you exit the Forbidden Journey, you are directed through a somewhat dimly lit shop inspired by the perpetually cranky caretaker, Mr. Filch.   As the name implies, this shop has a variety of items to purchase, such as Hogwarts and Quidditch clothing, toys, movie prop replicas, and another great example of "Muggle Magic," the Interactive Marauders Map, which includes a wand for use only on the map.   Also in this shop, at the attraction's exit, guests can purchase a photo of their ride experience on Harry Potter and the Forbidden Journey.

Flight of the Hippogriff

This is redesigned attraction is the last existing remnant of the Lost Continent, the area prior to the Hogsmeade's opening. Flight of the Hippogriff is the former children's coaster ride, the Flying Unicorn, which has been redesigned and re-themed.

Flight of the Hippogriff is a family friendly coaster based upon everyone's favorite feathered character, Buckbeak.   The actual coaster ride is very short, but what is even more worth the wait time are the views of Hogsmeade seen from the ride and the charming queue featuring Hagrid's cabin.   The ride is a great choice for those too small or timid to ride Forbidden Journey.   The coaster is just fast enough to be fun for all ages. As you climb the first hill remember to show the proper respect and bow to Buckbeak in his nest!

You must be 36 inches in height to ride. This family friendly ride is classified as a roller coaster and your seat is secured by a lap bar.

Wizard Trivia Question #5: What was the new name given to Buckbeak, the Hippogriff, when he was given back to Hagrid after Sirius' death?

The Three Broomsticks

In the book, Harry Potter and the Prisoner of Azkaban, Harry sneaks into Hogsmeade and sits in the back of the Three Broomsticks. It is in this same place that he develops his love for Butterbeer. This restaurant was actually completed before the Azkaban film was completed and the film sets were identical to this establishment. The atmosphere is complete with vaulted ceilings flanked by oak beams and dark furniture. If the weather is nice, additional seating is available outside overlooking the lake.

The menu is consists of hearty British fare as well as park favorites from the previous restaurant. Fish and chips (cod), Shepherd's pie (Harry's favorite), Cornish Pasty, chargrilled ribs, turkey legs, fresh vegetables and desserts complete the lunch and dinner menu. The restaurant also features a hearty breakfast menu. For more information, see Chapter 9: Fantastic Eats and Where to Find Them.

Wink: Shadows of House Elves are often seen in the rafters at this restaurant.

Butterbeer Keg Cart

One of the single most popular items at the Wizarding World is Butterbeer. Butterbeer from the large red cart is a rite of passage for Muggles visiting The Wizarding World of Harry Potter. The lines are so long at this cart that a second cart has been added to Hogsmeade. At this cart, you can purchase two varieties, frozen Butterbeer or the cream topped carbonated Butterbeer. In winter months, hot butterbeer is available.

The Magic Neep

Another open kiosk, Magic Neep is geared to Muggles who desire a healthy diet snack. This open air cart offers guests fresh fruits on ice, cold bottled water and pumpkin juice, and snacks to refresh and nourish in the hot Florida climate. If you look past it, you can see the Magic Neep store front.

Dervish and Banges

Before the opening of Diagon Alley, Muggles desiring wizarding and Quidditch equipment had one shop to explore. Dervish and Banges is still providing a wide range of magical supplies and wizarding equipment such as Sneakoscopes, Spectrespecs, Omnioculars, and The Monster Book of Monsters. If you are shopping for Quidditch supplies, Dervish and Bangs carries t-shirts, Quaffles, Golden Snitches and brooms including the Nimbus Two Thousand and One and the Firebolt. Hogwarts school uniforms and clothing including robes, scarves, ties, t-shirts and sweatshirts are also available at this store.

Honeydukes

A favorite of Muggles and Wizards is Hogsmeade's legendary sweetshop, Honeydukes. The shelves are lined with colorful sweets, including Acid Pops, Cauldron Cakes, Treacle Fudge, Fizzing Whizzbees, and the Muggle and Wizard favorite, Chocolate Frogs. These frogs not only contain a wizard trading card in each box, but are made with a special magical chocolate which is slow to melt in the hot Florida weather. Brave Muggles love to try Bertie Bott's Every-Flavour Beans with tasty (and not so tasty) flavours for you to discover!

Chocolate Frogs are a favorite treat which are also bought as souvenirs. The high quality chocolate is formulated so that it doesn't melt so quickly. This is great but the reason many collect these is that there are collectible Wizard cards in each box. The card collecting started with only four, the founders of Hogwarts, before more were added. New cards have recently been added in 2018. Here is a list of the available Chocolate Frog Cards:

Godric Gryffindor—Founder of Gryffindor House
Rowena Ravenclaw—Founder of Ravenclaw House
Helga Hufflepuff—Founder of Hufflepuff House
Salazar Slytherin—Founder of Slytherin House
Albus Dumbledore—particularly famous for his defeat of the Dark Wizard Grindelwald.
Gilderoy Lockhart—Wizarding Celebrity Author
Hengist of Woodcroft—founder of the Village of Hogsmeade
Bertie Bott—Creator of Bertie Bott's Every-Flavour Beans

The following are the two newest cards:

Jocunda Sykes—the first witch to fly over the Atlantic by broom.

Devlin Whitehorn—known for creating the Nimbus Racing Broom Company.

Wink: In 2014, an Undetectable Extension charm was placed on the shop as the inside was expanded to take over the inside space of Zonko's Joke Shop.

Owl Post

The Owl Post sells stationery, writing implements and owl toys and gifts, but what attracts most Muggles to this shop is that you can purchase The Wizarding World of Harry Potter™ stamps and you can actually mail letters with a special Hogsmeade™ postmark, a cool souvenir. The new Owl Post shipping and packaging is only available at the Diagon Alley location.

Ollivanders™

Ollivanders is a maker of fine wands since 382 B.C. In 2010, Mr. Ollivander opened this new location at Hogsmeade. He misjudged, however, how many Muggles would stand in line to step into the small dusty shop with wand boxes stacked to the ceiling for their chance to be chosen at the wand ceremony. There are very long lines at this location without the benefit of shade. As in Diagon Alley, the wand chooses the wizard. After the show, you can purchase your own individual Ollivanders wand, or choose from a selection including Harry Potter film character wands, collectible wands, interactive wands and replica wands (without Magic).

Hogsmeade™ Station

When guests are ready to depart Hogsmeade and travel to Diagon Alley, the best mode of travel is the Hogwarts Express to London. A Hogwarts Prefect will guide your party to a compartment aboard the Hogwarts Express. As you depart, through your "window," you'll encounter the irrepressible Weasley twins on broomstick advertising their shop in Diagon Alley. After admiring the scenic views of the British countryside from the train window, it won't be long before you get a glimpse of the Knight Bus before arriving at your London destination, Kings Cross Station.

FYI: Electric scooters are allowed on the train, but rented strollers must be turned in at the station and picked up at the next station. Remember, you must purchase a Park to Park Admission Ticket as this ride actually brings guests into a different park, Universal Studios. Ticket counters are next to the attraction to upgrade.

Hogsmeade Entertainment

On the "stage" located near Flight of the Hippogriff, periodic shows are performed inspired by several of the Harry Potter films.

The Frog Choir

A Hogwarts student announces The Frog Choir, an a-cappella singing group composed of four Hogwarts student singers and two singing frogs. The singing group is inspired by a scene in Harry Potter and the Prisoner of Azkaban.

During the 10 minute show, the group performs popular wizard favorites such as Something Wicked This Way Comes and Hedwig's Theme. The singers and frogs are available for photographs after the performance.

The Triwizard Spirit Rally

Inspired by the film, Harry Potter and the Goblet of Fire, The Triwizard Spirit Rally can be compared to a Muggle pep rally. The young men of Durmstrang Institute perform in an athletic and somewhat manly style, as they perform a coordinated "battle" with sticks, kicks and jumps to the Durmstrang theme. Next, the lovely ladies of Beauxbatons Academy of Magic arrive in their blue traveling cloaks to perform in a choreographed performance with batons and ribbons to their theme music.

The entire performance lasts about six minutes and the performers are available after for photographs.

Wink: With the closure of Dragon Challenge, this performance is now the only remaining remnant from the filmHarry Potter and the Goblet of Fire.

A New Attraction

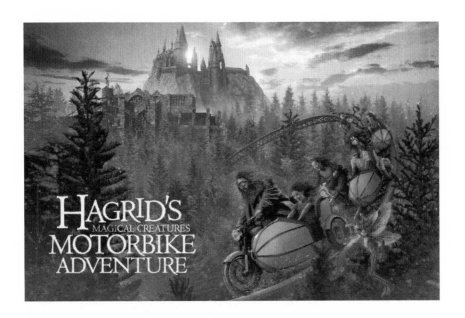

Dragon Challenge, a beloved original Islands of Adventure ride which was a set of two roller coasters closed in 2017. Nothing remains of the dueling dragons, but on this site, a new wizarding world attraction is under construction in Hogsmeade. On Hagrid's Magical Creatures Motorbike Adventure you fly far beyond the grounds of Hogwarts castle on a thrilling roller coaster ride that plunges into the paths of some of the wizarding world's rarest magical creatures. Hagrid's Magical Creatures Motorbike Adventure, Universal's most highly themed coaster opens June 13, 2019!

Harry Potter and the Escape from Gringotts was the last new attraction to open in the wizarding world. When the ride opened, the park was incredibly crowded and wait times for the new ride reached 6 hours! We can expect the same with this new coaster and perhaps even longer because this will attract coaster fans in addition to Harry Potter fans.

Universal Orlando cancelled the Celebration of Harry Potter in 2019, but we suspect this is because of an even bigger celebration which may take place when the new attraction opens!

"Oh, these people's minds work in strange ways, Petunia, they're not like you and me," said Uncle Vernon, trying to knock in a nail with the piece of fruitcake Aunt Petunia had just brought him."
Vernon Dursley
Harry Potter and the Sorcerer's Stone

6 MAKING MAGIC

Wizards throughout the world are astounded at the reversal of past standards of secrecy for the practice of magic near Muggles. Rumors circle the world of witchcraft and wizardry that the Confundus spell was placed on the Minister for Magic. Nevertheless, Muggles are allowed to practice a limited amount

of magic at Universal Orlando. The portraits in Dumbledore's office have certainly had much discussion of the merits or disastrous effects this decision will have. Salazar Slytherin's portrait is particularly disturbed at the sight of all these Muggles in Hogsmeade!

When The Wizarding World of Harry Potter—Hogsmeade opened in 2010, the wands only created magic for those with magical abilities. With the opening of Diagon Alley in 2014, Muggles are now allowed to purchase "interactive" wands. With such a wand, Muggles can cast simple spells with delightful effects.

Character wands are available which match the wand of your favorite witches and wizards from the books such as Harry, Hermione, Dumbledore and even the original wand of He Who Must Not Be Named! The Elder Wand may be purchased as well as many "unclaimed" wands waiting to choose their wizards.

Wink: The old "replica" wands are still for sale at a lower price than the interactive wands. These "non-magical" wands cost about $40 while the new interactive wands cost about $50 or more. The old wands are a great deal for actual Wizards and Witches!

Visiting Ollivander's shop in Diagon Alley is the best way for Muggles to learn information about wand lore. Ollivander's wands correspond to the Celtic Tree Calendar, as seen on the wall of the shop.

Wink: J. K. Rowling linked Harry, Ron and Hermione's wand to this calendar and now you can have this link too. Tell the attendants at Ollivander's your birthday and they will tell you which wand wood to purchase.

Wands are also available Ollivander's in Hogsmeade, at Wands by Gregorovitch in Diagon Alley, and at the Universal Store near the entrance at the theme parks.

Included with your new interactive wand is a two-sided map of the Wizarding World with spell locations. These maps lead you to brass medallion markers in the pavement which point to the spot of each spell. On the medallions as well as on the map is a diagram of how the spell should be cast. Of course, the clever Universal wizards have a few hidden spells, which are not on the maps.

Wink: There are secrets on your Spell Map which can only be revealed under the black light in Knockturn Alley.

Wink: To avoid frustration, study the map provided with your wand and this guide before you begin casting spells. Since Diagon Alley is so popular with Muggles, there is usually a line at each spot. The best time to cast spells in early in the morning or late afternoon when many Muggles have left the parks.

Wink: Diagon Alley is open during Halloween Horror Nights, a curious event for the scaring of Muggles (security measures are in place to keep out Death Eaters and Dementors). This is a great time to visit Diagon Alley, ride Harry Potter and the Escape from Gringotts and cast spells!

Casting Spells in Diagon Alley

Provided for you here is a list of magic spell locations with the corresponding spells to study before visiting Diagon Alley. This list does not intend to spoil the surprise of magic, but rather to prepare Muggles for their first attempt at magic. The spells have varying difficulty levels, but there is always a wizard team member nearby to assist (although not as many in Hogsmeade). Muggles get better at spell casting with practice. Because of the crowded conditions of Diagon Alley and Hogsmeade, knowing where to look for spells before your visit will be very helpful. Prepare to be delighted by your magical achievements.

Winks to help with Spell Casting:

• Stand directly behind the spell brass medallion.

• Hold your arm straight out at the target and flick from the wrist. Try not to move your arm.

- Ask a Wizard Team Member for help if you have difficulty achieving magic.

Horizont Alley Spell Locations

- Pilliwinkle's Playthings, Spell: Tarantallegra
- Flimflams Lanterns, Spell: Incendio
- Umbrella Sign, Spell: Meteolojinx
- Magical Menagerie, Spell: Silencio
- Wiseacres Wizarding Equipment, Spell: Dark Detectors
- Wiseacres Wizarding Equipment, Spell: Specialis Revelio
- Scribbulus, Spell: Wingardium Leviosa

Wink: Secret Spell Location
Scribbulus: In the window to the right of the Scribbulus shop door

Carkitt Market Spell Locations

- Brown E. Wright Blacksmith, Spell: Reparo
- Brown E. Wright Blacksmith, Spell: Locomotor Bellows
- Mermaid Fountain, Spell: Aguamenti

Diagon Alley Spell Locations

Weasley's Wizard Wheezes, Spell: Descendio

Wink: Secret Spell Location
There are two secret spell locations at Slug and Jigger's Apothecary

- In the apothecary window along Diagon Alley

- In the apothecary window along Diagon Alley (to the right of the prior spell)

Casting Spells in Knockturn Alley

- Chimney Sweep Elf Sign, Spell: Locomotor Chimney Sweep

• Dystyl Phaelanges, Spell: Moving Skeleton

• Noggin and Bonce, Spell: Mimblewimble

• Tallow and Hemp Toxic Tapers, Spell: Incendio

• Trackleshanks Locksmith, Spell: Alohomora

Casting Spells in Hogsmeade

Because Hogsmeade was originally built without the ability to cast spells, the modifications and the lack of space in throughout makes spell casting in Hogsmeade a little more difficult.

• Zonko's Joke Shop, Spell: Incendio

• McHavelocks, Spell: Arresto Momentum

• Honeyduke's, Spell: Revelio

• Dogweed and Deathcap, Spell: Herbivicus

• Gladrags Wizardwear, Spell: Asecendio/ Descendio

• Madam Puddifoots, Spell: Locomotor Snowman

• Dervish and Banges, Spell: Locomotor – Arresto Momentum

• Tome and Scrolls, Spell: Alohomora

• Spintwitches, Spell: Wingardium Leviosa

Wink: Casting spells in Hogsmeade may be a little more difficult because of the more crowded lanes. Originally, there were no spell locations in Hogsmeade. The shop windows have been reworked to include magical effects and there are not as many wizard team members on hand to help.

'He was a skinny, black-haired, bespectacled boy who had the pincer, slightly unhealthy look of someone who has grown a lot in a short space of time.'
Harry Potter and the Order of the Phoenix

7 A WIZARD'S JOURNEY THROUGH BOOKS AND FILMS

Muggles and Wizards express their delight at the first sight of the Wizarding World of Harry Potter. In this chapter, we follow Harry's footsteps as he discovered the wonders of Diagon Alley and Hogsmeade for the first time. Perhaps one day, Muggles will visit all of the places on Harry's journey, but for now, you can follow these directions to recreate for yourself a young wizard's journey into the world of magic.

Starting the Journey

To begin your wizard journey, arrive at the entrance gate at Universal Studios Florida 45 minutes prior to the posted opening time (to avoid the muggle crowds that build quickly). Walk straight through to the New York section and turn right when you see the Macy's storefront. Follow this lane through San Francisco all the way to the London waterfront.

In this section you'll see King's Cross Station, a record shop and book shop, Leicester Square Station, the Wyndham Theater, and Grimmauld Place. Look for a nondescript black door (muggles usually don't notice it) with the faded sign for The Leaky Cauldron.

In the first of the series of books about the famous young wizard, Harry Potter and the Sorcerer's Stone, Harry is brought to the Leaky Cauldron by Rubeus Hagrid, Hogwarts Keeper of the Keys.

Entering The Leaky Cauldron

Next to the Leaky Cauldron sign is a red building with the sign that reads "Leicester Square Station" and a large white building, the Wyndham Theater. Under these two buildings are several non-marked openings to Diagon Alley. Enter in the one nearest The Leaky Cauldron sign on the left and you'll soon see the opening in the bricks (it's permanently open so as to prevent muggle heart attacks at this first sight of magic).

Since this is a muggle resort, the magic is limited, but with your first step into Diagon Alley, like Harry, you'll wish you had eight more eyes! It is truly magical with the sights, sounds, and smells of a wizard village. You won't see any theme park rides or American soda advertisements here.

On your left is the actual entrance to The Leaky Cauldron. Harry actually went here before entering Diagon Alley. Step inside and bask in the atmosphere! Order a traditional English breakfast of eggs, sausage, black pudding, bacon, beans and potatoes or the egg, leak and mushroom pasty. Come back for lunch and try the Ploughman's Lunch, Bangers and Mash or Cottage Pie. If you're thirsty, there are several non-alcoholic beverages such as Butterbeer, Fishy Green Ale, and Otter's Fizzy Orange Juice; or try one of two exclusive beers only available in Diagon Alley, Dragon Scale and Wizard's Brew.

Wizard Trivia Question #6: On which London lane is the Leaky Cauldron located?

Exchanging Muggle Money

Your next stop is Gringotts Money Exchange which is next to the attraction, Harry Potter and the Escape from Gringotts. Walk straight down the lane; it is impossible to miss the impressive Gringotts building (curiously one of the dragons must have gotten loose and is sitting atop it). To stick to Harry's timely journey, you can ask the attendant to tour the ride queue at this time, or visit the ride later. Walk to the right of the bank building to Gringotts Money Exchange. You can speak to the goblin on duty and exchange your dollars for some Wizarding Bank Notes with which to do your shopping in the wizarding world.

Wizard trivia question #7: How much is a gold Galleon worth?

Madam Malkin's Robes for All Occasions

It is time to get your wizard robes and Madam Malkin's Robes for All Occasions is the place to do it. Head back toward The Leaky Cauldron and enter the purple store front. Muggles can use their currency to purchase Hogwarts school uniforms, scarves, ties, robes and accessories of their favorite Hogwarts houses, Gryffindor, Ravenclaw, Hufflepuff and Slytherin.

Wizard Trivia Question #8: For what purpose are horned slugs useful?

There are several stops on Harry's journey that are not open to the general public (but magic happens in their windows). Next on Harry's journey is across the lane at the green store front of Flourish and Blott's. This is where Hogwarts students buy school text books. The store front of Pottages Cauldron Shop is next to Madam Malkin's with the very tall stack of cauldrons in front. The Apothecary where Harry got his potion ingredients is down the lane a few steps.

Wizard trivia question #9: In the film, Harry Potter and the Sorcerer's Stone, which two names were on either side of James Potter on the Gryffindor plaque in the trophy case?

Magical Menagerie

Eyelops Owl Emporium has unfortunately gone out of business but you can buy plush owls like Hedwig and Pigwidgeon as well as a variety of other creatures including Crookshanks, Fang, Buckbeak, Fluffy and Scabbers at Magical Menagerie. Also available are Cornish pixies, ferrets, and Pygmy Puffs.

Wizard Trivia question #10: What kind of owl is Harry's Hedwig?

The Wand Chooses the Wizard

The first item that all young wizards and witches are eager

to buy is their magic wand. Wands are of extreme importance in the wizarding world and finding the right wand is a tricky business. The next stop on this wizard's journey is Ollivanders, Makers of Fine Wands since 382 BC.

In this shop, the wand chooses the wizard. During each "show" a lucky guest is chosen by the wizard on duty. The guest will be instructed to cast a variety of spells with different wands until the perfect one is found. It is a must-see experience on your magical journey.

As you exit, you'll enter the wand shop to choose your own. Choose an "interactive wand" made especially for Muggles which will perform safe amounts of magic in Diagon Alley and Hogsmeade. Wave your wand, recite the spell, and watch as the magic unfolds!

Wizard trivia question #11: What substances does Ollivander use as the magical core to his wands?

All Aboard the Hogwarts Express

Exit Diagon Alley and return to the London Waterfront for the next phase of Harry's journey. Enter King's Cross Station. A muggle attendant is there to greet you and check your park to park pass for admission to board. Wind your way through the corridors until you see Platforms 9 and 10. You'll walk straight through a solid brick wall (or at least it will look like it to the muggles behind you) onto Platform 9 ¾. You will feel the same sense of awe that Harry felt at his first glimpse of the Hogwarts Express! Wind your way around wizards trunks and owl cages (look for Hedwig) to boarding lanes, where a Hogwarts Prefect will be waiting to lead you to your passenger compartment.

Wizard Trivia Question #12: How many uses for dragon's blood did Dumbledore discover?

The Wizards' Academy

To follow Harry's journey, exit the Hogwarts Express to your right and head straight to the iconic Hogwarts Castle. To specifically follow this timeline, tell the attraction attendant that you are only doing the Castle Tour. The ride associated with this attraction has many elements from later books, and we wouldn't want to jump ahead.

On the tour, you'll begin in the dungeons, travel through the gallery of portraits and witness a conversation between the founders of Hogwarts. You'll visit Dumbledore's office and see the sorting hat. Next is the Griffindor Common Room, but you'll have to get past the Fat Lady's portrait. Other features on the tour are the Defense Against the Dark Arts classroom and the Room of Requirement. Hagrid's Cabin is nearby but you can wait to see it later when you'll also meet Buckbeak, the hippogriff.

At the end of the first book, head back to London on the Hogwarts Express to Kings Cross Station.

Wizard Trivia Question #13: Who was the first owner of the Sorting Hat?

Creepy and Cool

In the second book, Harry Potter and the Chamber of Secrets, Harry is rescued from the Dursleys by the Weasley brothers in an enchanted Ford Anglia. This car was found in the ride queue of Dragon Challenge but this attraction is now closed. Harry is brought to the Burrow to spend the rest of his vacation with the Weasleys. Mrs. Weasley enjoys listening to Celestina Warbeck on Wizard Radio. Return to Diagon Alley to watch Celestina perform in the Carkitt Market area of Diagon Alley.

When Harry and the Weasley's go to Diagon Alley to purchase school supplies, Harry takes a wrong turn when he travels through the Floo Network for the first time and lands in Knockturn Alley. Knockturn Alley is darker, colder and creepier than the rest of the park because of its focus on the Dark Arts. It has only one shop, Borgin and Bourkes. As you would expect, the shop is filled with dark objects and sinister items but you don't have to be a Death Eater to gain entry to this infamous shop.

Luckily, you won't need Hagrid to lead you out of Knockturn Alley. Just follow the path until you see the light. Harry would then buy his school supplies in Diagon Alley and head back to Hogwarts Castle on the Hogwarts Express. Skip this step for now and exit Diagon Alley and enter the London Waterfront area.

Wizard Trivia Question #14: What is Moaning Myrtle's full name?

The third book in the series is Harry Potter and the Prisoner of Azkaban. Harry leaves the Dursleys and heads to London on a magical form of transport.

Wizard Travel by Bus

The Knight Bus is parked on the London waterfront area. It's a big purple, triple-decker bus straight out of the movie. If you notice strangely dressed Muggles speaking to the attendant, these are probably wizards in a poor disguise trying to arrange transport back to London. Passers-by can look in the windows and see curtains, beds, and an ornate chandelier. Have a conversation with the talkative shrunken head hanging over the steering wheel and the Knight Bus conductor. They might let you have a look inside.

After Harry escapes the Dursleys via the Knight Bus, he heads to the Leaky Cauldron where he spends the rest of his summer until school starts. To follow Harry on his wizard's journey, spend some time in Diagon Alley.

One of Harry's favorite shops is Quality Quidditch Supplies where you will find everything you will need to play the most popular sport in the wizarding world! The shop carries an assortment of Quidditch apparel and equipment including Quidditch sweaters, brooms, Golden Snitches, Bludgers, and Quaffles!

Beat the Heat with a Sweet Treat

If you are ready for a sweet treat that will beat the savage Florida heat, head to Florean Fortescue's Ice Cream Parlour. This is where Harry spent every afternoon of his summer in Diagon Alley, sitting at a table to do his summer homework.

Magical displays of ice-cream cones welcome guests into this colorful, quaint ice-cream parlour where patrons may enjoy hand-scooped and soft-serve ice-creams. Continental breakfast items and pastries are available in the morning hours along with bottled Pumpkin Juice, teas and water. Try such ice cream flavours as Butterbeer, Earl Grey and Lavender, toffee apple and Harry's favorite, peanut butter and strawberry.

Next on his journey, Harry heads back to Hogwarts Castle on the Hogwarts Express train. In this book, he meets Buckbeak, the hippogriff and he uses his invisibility cloak to visit magical places that might tempt your tastebuds.

Tip: Stop at a merchandise cart in Hogsmeade and purchase a Timeturner just like the one that Professor McGonagall gave to Hermione.

Visiting Buckbeak

Buckbeak, everyone's favorite Hippogriff, has the head and wings of an eagle and the body of a horse. You can visit Buckbeak and see Hagrid's cabin on the ride, Flight of the Hippogriff. This is a family friendly coaster that turns and dives around the pumpkin patch, and swoops past Hagrid's hut. Be sure to bow to Buckbeak on your way up the track! Although a short ride, it has fantastic views of Hogsmeade. You must be 36 inches in height to ride this small roller coaster.

Marauder's Map

While at school, the Weasley twins give Harry the Marauders' Map which they swiped from the caretaker, Mr. Filch's office. He then uses the map to visit Hogsmeade by way of secret passages.

Secret passages are hidden from Muggles in Orlando, but if you want a Marauder's Map, visit Filch's Emporium of Confiscated Goods at the base of Hogwarts castle. Magical "interactive" Marauder's Maps which let the viewer follow the footsteps of Dumbledore, Snape, Harry, Ron and Hermione are available. The interactive map comes with a special wand whose magic works only on the map.

When Harry emerges from the secret passageway, he finds himself in the delightful haven of sweet delights, Honeydukes, home to tempting treats that delight wizards tastebuds! Visit Honeydukes to purchase some of these tasty treats.

Under cover of his invisibility cloak, Harry enters the Three Broomsticks to listen in on a conversation. In Hogsmeade, the Three Broomsticks is a dining establishment where you can choose from British delicacies such as fish and chips, Cornish pasty and Harry's favorite, Shepherds Pie.

The Castle

Head back to Hogwarts castle and ride Harry Potter and the Forbidden Journey. This is certainly an intense magical experience combining video with actual props. Soar above the castle grounds as you join Harry Potter and his friends on an unforgettably thrilling adventure! This amazing attraction utilizes groundbreaking Kuka Arm technology (and a little magic) to create a one-of-a-kind ride experience. You'll come face to face with giant spiders, Dementors and lots more as you learn the castle's secret!

Challenge of Champions

Muggles are hoping that someday, they might attend the wizard Quidditch World Cup at Universal Orlando. Visit Dervish and Banges for Quidditch supplies. More supplies are available at Quality Quidditch Supplies in Diagon Alley.

Before the Triwizard Tournament begins, Harry and the other champions are interviewed by Rita Skeeter, reporter for the Daily Prophet. Their office is in Diagon Alley. Knock on the Daily Prophet door or use the door knocker and listen for a reply behind the door.

Wizard Trivia Question #15: What was Cedric Diggory's Quidditch position?

There are a few other references to Harry Potter and the Goblet of Fire. Hermione's Yule Ball gown is in a shop window in Hogsmeade and also at Madam Malkin's in Diagon Alley.

Back in Hogsmeade, enquire as to when you can catch performances in Hogsmeade of the Triwizard Spirit Rally. Cheer on the colorful procession of students from Hogwarts, the lovely dancing ladies of Beauxbatons, and the strong young men of Durmstrang Academy as they lead the excitement for the Triwizard Tournament.

When back in Diagon Alley, notice the Mermaid statue in Carkitt Market which reminds us of the underwater challenge in the Triwizard Tournament.

The Home of Black Magic

In book number five, Harry Potter and the Order of the Phoenix, Harry leaves the Dursley's with the help of a few aurors. He arrives at Number 12 Grimmauld Place in London, the home of Sirius Black and headquarters of the Order of the Phoenix. As you enter the London waterfront area, look to the brown brick buildings to the right and find number 12. Stand back and look up at the second floor window for a glimpse of Kreacher, the Black family house elf.

While in London, wander over to the red phone booth which represents the visitor entrance to the Ministry of Magic. Step inside the booth and dial the word, "Magic," to be connected to the Ministry of Magic.

By this time, you know that Harry will travel back to Hogwarts for his fifth year at Hogwarts on the train. As you exit the Hogwarts Express in Hogsmeade notice the invisible Thestral and carriage which carries students to Hogwarts Castle from the station.

During this year, Harry forms Dumbledore's Army, from a group of Hogwarts students. Their first meeting is at the Hogs Head Pub. This pub is adjacent to The Three Broomsticks and is an excellent place to enjoy a Butterbeer or Fire Whisky.

On the way back from a snowy visit to Hogsmeade, fellow Hogwarts student, Katie Bell, is cursed by an opal necklace which was meant for Dumbledore. You can see the cursed necklace at Borgin and Burkes in Knockturn Alley.

Dark Magic and Wizard Wheezes

In Harry's sixth year at Hogwarts and the adventure known as Harry Potter and the Half Blood Prince, the first place to visit at Universal Orlando is Weasley's Wizard Wheezes in Diagon Alley. One would have to admit that this is the most iconic spot in Diagon Alley, second only to Gringotts.

Wizard Trivia Question #16: What is Weasley's Wizard Wheezes address?

While shopping in Diagon Alley, Ron, Hermione and Harry follow Draco to Knockturn Alley and watch through a window as Draco examines a mysterious cabinet. You can find this cabinet at Borgin and Bourkes in Knockturn Alley.

Wizard Trivia Question #17: What is the name of the potion known as "Liquid Luck?"

Wizard Trivia Question #18: What is the name of the vampire who attends Professor Slughorn's party.

The Dragon Escapes

The seventh book in J. K. Rowling's series, Harry Potter and the Deathly Hallows starts out with Voldemort's banquet at Malfoy Manor. This location is not really on Harry's journey, but you do get a glimpse of its sinister setting on the Hogwarts Express train ride.

When Harry leaves the Dursleys' house for the last time, it is with a crew of decoy Harry's. The real Harry rides in the sidecar of Sirius' enchanted motorbike. Go to Hogsmeade in Islands of Adventure to ride Hagrid's Magical Creatures Motorbike Adventure opening on June 13, 2019.

Wizard Trivia Question #19: Who is Tonks cousin?

While Harry, Ron and Hermione are in hiding, they realize that they must visit the Lovegood home. There Harry learns the story of the Deathly Hallows. In the Carkitt Market section of Diagon Alley, watch the puppet show of the same name. You can also see a magical creature of which Luna spoke on the upper floor of Magical Menagerie on Horizont Alley.

Wizard trivia question #20: For what purpose is essence of Dittany used?

On Harry's search for horcruxes, the Harry, Ron and Hermione decide to break into Bellatrix Lestrange's vault at Gringotts.

Head to Gringotts bank, the most iconic landmark in Diagon Alley. Enter the bank lobby and proceed to the ride, Harry Potter and the Escape from Gringotts where you and Bill Weasley will encounter Harry, Ron and Hermione's on their quest for a horcrux. Watch out for Bellatrix Lestrange and Voldemort's curses.

Wizard Trivia Quest #21: What is Dolores Umbridge's middle name?

Harry's journey through J. K. Rowling's books culminates at Hogwarts Castle with the Battle of Hogwarts. Several years later, Harry, Jenny, Ron and Hermione meet again at Platform 9 3/4 to send off their children for their journey to Hogwarts.

Wizard Trivia Question #22: What stones are encrusted in the Sword of Gryffindor?

"Yeah, we'll call you," muttered Ron as the knight disappeared, "if we ever need someone mental."
Ron Weasley
Harry Potter and the Prisoner of Azkaban

8 CELEBRATIONS AND SECRETS

Wizards and witches love celebrations as much as any Muggle. It is no different at the Wizarding World of Harry Potter. Although the controlling witch, Ms. Rowling, who retains creative control over the "world" banned Christmas celebrations in the early years, but now the wizarding world has its own Christmas celebration with a feast and decorations.

Christmas in the Wizarding World of Harry Potter

Christmas in The Wizarding World of Harry Potter™ debuted in 2017 in both Hogsmeade and Diagon Alley. To the delight of Harry Potter fans, the celebration features holiday decorations, special holiday treats and drinks, Christmas themed shows by the Frog Choir and Celestina Warbeck and nightly light shows at Hogwarts Castle.

Tip: During cool months, order a hot Butterbeer to sip while watching the nightly light show at Hogwarts Castle!

Orlando Informer's Private Events

From time to time, the Orlando Informer blog and website hosts a private function at The Wizarding World of Harry Potter™ — Hogsmeade™ and Diagon Alley. This is a fantastic way to tour without the crowds! These events have been expanded to include other areas of the parks. The festivities begin after both parks close to the general public. Unlimited non-alcoholic beverages are included including Butterbeer and also served is ice cream from Florean Fortescue's Ice Cream Parlour! Only a limited number of tickets are sold at these private events to keep the lines short and less crowded.

For information on future events, "Like" the Orlando Informer Facebook page, or join their Facebook group. Register for emails at www.orlandoinformer.com.

Secrets and Winks

Muggles remind us to stop and smell the roses, or at Universal Orlando, take in the details. The House Elves at Universal have added little hidden details which Muggles refer to as "Easter Eggs" or "Hidden Mickeys" (at Walt Disney World). Since Winky, the House Elf, hid most of them, I like to refer to them as Winks.

At the Wizarding World of Harry Potter, some of these winks are nods to past attractions. I won't give them all away, but here are a few hidden (or not so hidden) details that are not so obvious unless you are looking for them.

Spoiler Alert: if you would like to discover these Winks on your own, read no further! Don't worry, I'll leave a few for you to discover on your own.

A Few Winks at Hogsmeade

Since the Village of Hogsmeade is a little older, having opened in 2010, most of the Winks have been discovered by Muggles. A few changes came into effect when spell locations were added in the shop windows around Hogsmeade. Here are a few Winks to be found in Hogsmeade.

• At The Three Broomsticks, look for shadows of House Elves in the rafters.

• Inside the Public Conveniences (which Americans refer to as restrooms), Listen for Moaning Myrtle.

• While not so "hidden," look up at the clock tower. Instead of the normal clock chimes, an owl "hoots" every quarter hour.

• While sitting in the covered bench area near the Owl Post, look up to see several animatronic owls. Luckily the droppings are only for show.

• Hermione's Yule Ball gown is seen in the second story window at Gladrags Wizardwear in Hogsmeade.

• As you exit the Hogwarts Express station in Hogsmeade, a Hogwarts moving carriage is waiting to bring returning students to Hogwarts. Can you see the Thestrel harnessed to it?

Winks at the London Waterfront

• Kreacher often peeks out of the window at 12 Grimmauld Place, the home of Sirius Black.

• At Kings Cross Station, as you head to Platform 9 3/4, there are several winks to notice. Upon entering, notice the "London" chill in the air. Don't be in such a hurry that you miss reading the advertisements. The best one is the Divine Magic perfume billboard reminiscent of the one in front of which Dumbledore appeared to Harry in the film Harry Potter and the Half Blood Prince.

A Few Winks at Diagon Alley

When Diagon Alley opened in 2014, Muggles were amazed at the fire breathing dragon, wizard shops, and casting spells. It takes a few visits to this shopping district to notice all of the

Winks that were placed there.

- On Horizont Alley, you'll find Scribbulus Writing Implements. In Scribbulus' shop windows, one of the spell locations on the wand map is in the left shop window. However a secret spell location is found in the window to the right of the door.

- At Magical Menagerie, a shop full of plush animals found within the books and films, notice the alley to the left of the store. In the window is Nagini, the large pet snake and Horcrux of "He Who Must Not Be Named."

- Also at Magical Menagerie, look up for Luna Lovegood's favorite, the Crumple-Horned Snorkack, and several other magical creatures on the second level.

- The sign outside the Leaky Cauldron actually leaks.

Knockturn Alley Winks

At Borgin and Burkes there are several Winks to discover. Several of Voldemort's Horcruxes are displayed and the cursed necklace from the film, Harry Potter and the Half Blood Prince, is in a glass case. Also on display, is the Hand of Glory which grabbed Harry in the film, Harry Potter and the Chamber of Secrets. Draco's Vanishing Cabinet is also here (perk up your ears when near it).

Remembering Jaws

Many Muggles were in quite a snit upon learning that their beloved original park attraction, Jaws, was going to be replaced by Diagon Alley. In respect for the memory of Jaws, not only has the giant great white hanging shark, affectionately named "Bruce," been moved to the San Francisco area in Universal Studios (adjacent to the London Waterfront), but a few Winks have also been placed in Diagon Alley.

- In the window of the Record shop on the London waterfront is a record titled "Here's to Swimming' with Bowlegged Women" by the Quint Trio which was sung drunkenly by actors in the Jaws film.

- Telescopes inside Wiseacre's Gift Shop are made with pieces of old boats from the Jaws ride.

- A shark's jaw is seen inside the window of the Apothecary shop.

- A group on singing shrunken heads in Knockturn Alley occasionally sing a familiar tune from the film, Jaws.

"Percy wouldn't recognize a joke if it danced naked in front of him wearing Dobby's tea cozy."
Ron Weasley
Harry Potter and the Goblet of Fire

9 FANTASTIC EATS AND WHERE TO FIND THEM

Experiencing the magic of the Wizarding World of Harry Potter is an exhilarating experience, but can also be exhausting and can make wizards and Muggles quite hungry and thirsty. Luckily, Harry and friends have always found the tastiest of victuals when it is time for repast.

When building The Wizarding World of Harry Potter at Universal Orlando that clever British witch, J. K. Rowling, insisted on there being a distinctly British influence. American wizards are forbidden from advertising their Muggle money-making products in the wizarding world. If you want American brands of soda or merchandise, you will have to exit the Wizarding World and visit other areas.

There are three areas in the Wizarding World of Harry Potter in which to find refreshments: Hogsmeade, Diagon Alley and the London Waterfront.

Wizard Trivia Question #23: At what location was Harry when he first learned that Sirius Black was his Godfather?

The London Waterfront Eats

Outside of Diagon Alley in the London Waterfront area, there are two Cab Shelters which offer merchandise for sale and

British street fare. Enjoy several varieties of "Jacket Potatoes" and packets of crisps (baked potatoes and potato chips to Americans).

London Taxi Hut

Cab shelters are a familiar site in London. These were constructed in Victorian times to provide low cost meals and shelter for London Cab Men.

In more recent times, these shelters have been converted for the purpose of selling wares. At Universal, the London Taxi Hut menu provides some of Britain's favorite street fare, jacket potatoes (more commonly known as baked potatoes) with a variety of toppings which makes them a hearty meal. Also available is a theme park staple, the hot dog, and Golden Wonder Potato Crisps (known as potato chips in the United States).

Menu
Hot Dog with Crisps $12.99
Jacket Potato with beans and cheese $8.79
Jacket Potato with broccoli and cheese $8.79
Shepherd's Pie Jacket Potato $8.79
Loaded Jacket Potato $8.79
Crisps $3.50
Drinks:
Bottled Tea $4.49
Bottled Juice $4.49
Bottled Water $4.50
Canned Beer $7.99

King's Cross Station

Since you might need refreshment on your journey to Hogsmeade (the Trolley Witch is not available to Muggles), a small food and beverage booth has been place inside King's Cross Station in the queue for the Hogwarts Express. Crisps and candy are available in addition to the following prepared selections:

Fruit and Cheese Platter $7.99
A selection of assorted fruits, cheeses and crackers.
Hummus Tray $6.99
Classic style hummus served with sliced pita bread, celery and carrot sticks.
Fruit Plate $7.99
A large helping of a variety of fruit including sliced melon, pineapple, and grapes.
Ham and Cheese Sandwich $9.99
Honey-roasted ham and Swiss cheese is served on a white bread roll with Dijon mustard on the side with a bag of crisps.

Dining in Diagon Alley

When Harry entered the world of magic, one of the best surprises was the fantastic food! After living with the Dursley's for 10 years and sometimes practically starved, the wonderful meals were literally the cherry on top of the pudding!

At Diagon Alley, many examples of British fare are available in hearty dishes. Muggles have enjoyed some of these favorites in Hogsmeade but there are different choices available in Diagon Alley.

Quenching Thirst

The heat of the Florida can cause a mighty thirst whether witch, wizard, or Muggle. While Butterbeer has gained great popularity, there are several magical concoctions for satisfying the thirsty palette. These beverages can be found at several locations in both Diagon Alley and Hogsmeade.

Pumpkin Juice

Pumpkin Juice may have been the first "juice" Harry was served when he arrived at Hogwarts Castle for the first time. This sweet juice is available in unmistakable bottles around the Wizarding World with a pumpkin lid. The pumpkin flavour has touches of winter spices such as cinnamon and cloves. Some say the pumpkin juice on tap at the Hogs Head Pub is better than the bottled version.

Butterbeer

In Harry Potter and the Prisoner of Azkaban, Harry developed his love of Butterbeer. This foamy brew truly tastes of the magic of the wizarding world with hints of butterscotch, caramel, cream soda with a layer of whipped cream atop its sugary and fizzy sweetness. The frozen variety has the same butterscotch flavoured goodness in a slushy frozen concoction. For a short time during the year when the weather turns cooler, don't miss trying out Hot Butterbeer when it is offered. Butterbeer is served in a plastic cup or in a souvenir mug.

Wink: There are six different ways to enjoy the Butterbeer flavour.

Original Butterbeer
Frozen Butterbeer
Hot Butterbeer (seasonal)
Butterbeer ice cream (at Florean Fortescue's)
Butterbeer fudge (at Sugarplum's)
Butterbeer Potted Cream (at Leaky Cauldron).

Tongue Tying Lemon Squash

Sometimes, the simplicity of lemonade is magical and refreshing. This very tart lemonade drink with a hint of vanilla is served over ice with the addition of added fresh-squashed lemon, squashed just for you which add just enough citrus to temporarily "tie the tongue."

Peachtree Fizzing Tea

This peachy and slightly fizzy iced tea is quite possibly the best thirst quencher available. The light peach flavour with a hint of ginger slightly sweetens the tea and is a great alternative to some of the other overly sweet beverages.

Fishy Green Ale

This cloudy light green drink is one of the most interesting of all wizard drinks. The lightly carbonated drink has a distinct minty flavour and a hint of cinnamon but that's not all. Filling the bottom of the tall cup are blueberry pearl-sized bubbles which require a special black straw wide enough to slurp up these magic pearls!

Otter's Fizzy Orange Juice

You can thank Fred and George Weasley for the invention

of this fun fizzy fruity drink which is yet another of the Weasley brothers smashing success. A favorite of Diagon Alley, it has hint of vanilla and an orange slice.

Witches and Wizard's Brews

It's no surprise that the Universal wizards decided to create two exclusive beer brews for Diagon Alley (there are also exclusive brews in Hogsmeade). These specialty brews are craft beers, magically brewed and bursting with flavour. These are available for about $10 and served in a tall cup.

Dragon Scale, as the name would have it, is a fiery brew and is the lighter of the two brews. While being a little strong on the malt flavour, it is the more preferred beer of Muggles. The dark Wizard's Brew might have had an origin in Knockturn Alley due to its porter darkness. It is the sweeter of the two beers. These two brews are available at the Leaky Cauldron, The Hopping Pot, and Fountain of Fair Fortune.

The Leaky Cauldron

Hagrid's favorite pub, The Leaky Cauldron, is now open to hungry Muggles from all over the world. It is a combination of witty decor and satisfying meals. Breakfast, lunch and dinner are served at this fine establishment which feature staples of British fare and a few American favorites.

At this quick service restaurant, meals are ordered first and guests are then seated by the attending wizards. Take in the great decor and details while you wait for your meal to arrive at your table.

The Leaky Cauldron is open for breakfast (often frequented by Universal guests who have purchased a vacation package) which is usually served until 10:00 am.

Leaky Cauldron Menus

Breakfast
Includes small beverage

Traditional Breakfast - $16.99
Fresh scrambled eggs, sausage links, black pudding, English bacon, baked beans, grilled tomato, sautéed mushrooms and breakfast potatoes

Pancake Breakfast - $16.99
Three fluffy buttermilk pancakes, crisp bacon and link sausage with butter croissant

American Breakfast - $16.99
Fresh scrambled eggs, breakfast potatoes, crisp bacon, and link sausage with butter croissant

Apple Oatmeal Flan with Yogurt & Fruit - $16.99
Freshly baked flan of apples and oatmeal served with yogurt and fresh seasonal fruit

**Egg, Leek, & Mushroom Pasty - $16.99
Pastry wrapped scrambled eggs, mushrooms and leeks served with breakfast potatoes and fresh fruit

Kid's Breakfast - $12.39
Choose traditional, pancake or American

Beverages

Pumpkin Juice™ - $4.49
Hot Tea - $2.49
Fresh Brewed Coffee - $2.49
Apple Juice - $2.49
Orange Juice - $2.49
Milk - $2.69

Lunch And Dinner Menu

Entrées

Ploughman's - $21.99 Serves 2
Fish & Chips - $15.99
**Bangers & Mash - $12.99
Toad in the Hole - $10.99
Beef, Lamb & Guinness Stew - $14.99
**Cottage Pie - $14.99
Fisherman's Pie - $15.99
Mini Pie Combination - $15.49
Soup & Salad - $10.49

Sandwiches
Served with wedge fries

Banger - $12.99
Specialty Chicken - $12.99

Kids' Entrées

Macaroni Cheese - $6.99
Fish & Chips - $6.99
Mini Pie - $6.99

Beverages

Butterbeer™ - $6.99
Frozen Butterbeer™ - $6.99
Pumpkin Juice™ - $4.99
Tongue Tying Lemon Squash - $5.49
Otter's Fizzy Orange Juice - $5.49
Fishy Green Ale - $5.49
Peachtree Fizzing Tea - $5.49
Gillywater - $4.50
Draught Beer

Wizard's Brew $8.99
Dragon Scale $8.99
Draught Beer $8.99
Whisky - $8.99
Fire Whisky
Wine By The Glass - $7.00

Desserts

Sticky Toffee Pudding - $7.49
Cranachan - $6.99
Butterbeer™ Potted Cream - $5.79
Chocolate Potted Cream - $4.69

Florean Fortescue's Ice Cream Parlour

As the Florida heat intensifies, a stop in at Harry's favorite ice cream parlour is exactly what the doctor ordered. Florean's offers a unique array of flavours in soft serve and hand packed ice creams.

The showpiece flavour the striped soft serve Butterbeer Ice Cream. Florean Fortescue's Ice-Cream Parlour appeared in

Harry Potter and the Prisoner of Azkaban when Mr. Fortescue himself gave Harry free ice cream sundaes every half hour. Ice cream is served here in cups, waffle cones, and plastic souvenir sundae glasses.

Flavours include hard packed ice cream and soft serve. The soft serve has a magical element which creates a striped effect for extra flavour. Single orders can contain two different flavours, and you can add unusual toppings like shortbread crumbles and meringue pieces.

Features

Butterbeer Ice Cream
Served in a cup $5.49
Served in a waffle cone $5.99
Served in a souvenir glass $7.49

Chocolate Strawberry Peanutbutter Sundae
Strawberry Peanutbutter Ice Cream with hot fudge, whipped cream and shortbread crumbles served in a souvenir glass $8.49

Soft Serve

Banana, chocolate, mint, Granny Smith, pistachio, vanilla, orange marmalade, toffee, toffee apple, strawberries & cream
Served in a cup $5.49
Served in a waffle cone $5.99
Served in a souvenir glass $7.49

Hand Packed

Chocolate Chili, Apple Crumble, Vanilla, Salted Caramel Blondie, Chocolate, Clotted Cream, Earl Grey and Lavender, Sticky Toffee Pudding, Chocolate and Raspberry, Strawberry and Peanutbutter

Served in a cup $6.49

Served in a waffle cone $6.99
Served in a souvenir glass $8.49

Sundaes $7.49
With whipped cream and a cherry
Hot Fudge, Hot Caramel, Strawberry topping

Toppings $0.99

Shortbread crumbles
Waffle cone pieces
crystals
Chocolate chips
chopped nuts

Wizard Trivia Question #24: What flavour ice cream did Hagrid bring to Harry on his first visit Diagon Alley?

The Hopping Pot

The Hopping Pot, named for a story from The Tales of Beedle the Bard, is a walk-up pub style bar with counter service and picnic tables. This is a good place to grab a beverage and snack if the weather is nice. Take a seat at one of the tables to enjoy your refreshments and enjoy one of the magical songstress, Celestina Warbeck or one the Tales of Beedle the Bard shows.

The Hopping Pot Menu:

Non-Alcoholic Drinks

Butterbeer™
Frozen Butterbeer™
Tongue Tying Lemon Squash
Otter's Fizzy Orange Juice

Fishy Green Ale
Peachtree Fizzing Tea
Pumpkin Juice™
Gillywater

Alcoholic Drinks

Wizard's Brew
Dragon Scale
Draught Beer
Fire Whiskey

Food

Beef Pasties

Fountain of Fair Fortune

This little counter is named after a story in The Tales of Beedle the Bard is a great stop for quick refreshment. The menu includes:

Butterbeer, Frozen Butterbeer, Fishy Green Ale, Gilly Water, Wizard's Brew, Dragon Scale and Draught Beer

Eternelle's Elixirs of Refreshment

Eternelle's is a gothic themed kiosk in Carkitt Market where wizards and Muggles can purchase an elixir for the quenching of thirst with magical additives. Each corner of the kiosk is flanked at the top by busts of rather frightening magical beings: Basilisk, hippogriff, Dementor, thestral, dragon, and a werewolf.

At this kiosk, bottled Gilly Water (which tastes and looks the same as Muggle bottled water) with an authentic wizarding world themed label can be purchased for $4.00 You might also care to choose between four different magical elixirs of different colors to transform the water into a magical potion for $4.50.

Fire Protection Potion: Orange in color; the refreshing flavours of watermelon, peach and strawberry will cool the tongue.

Babbling Beverage: Red in color; the blend of tropical fruit flavours will elicit exclamations of joy.

Draught of Peace: Blue in color; the flavours of mixed berries including blueberry and raspberry bring a calming sensation to your palette.

Elixir to Induce Euphoria: Green in color; the flavours of pineapple and apples bring happiness to a hot day.

Weasley's Wizard Wheezes

The highly successful Weasley brothers began their career with creative propensity for pranks disguised as sweets (much to Dudley's despair). The most popular of their sweets promises to make the student appear ill to escape class. The brothers have promised that all goods sold in Diagon Alley are safe for Muggle consumption, but be sure to read the warning labels on the box, just in case a charmed box of sweets has magical results when consumed.

Fainting Fancies: Large round citrus flavoured gummy candies coated in sugar.

Nosebleed Nougat: Milk chocolate covered marshmallow topped with pistachios and white candy coated chocolate balls.

Puking Pastilles: The box describes them as "hard boiled sweets," however they are diamond shaped green and purple sticky candy.

Fever Fudge: Vanilla flavoured fudge embedded with fiery jelly beans.

U-No-Poo: Green in color, these are candy coated chocolate discs.

Skiving Snackbox $39.99.   The Weasley's most famous and exclusive sweets assortment is the Skiving Snackbox. It includes four types of candy: Fainting Fancies, Nosebleed Nuggets, Fever Fudge, and Puking Pastilles.

Gringott's Money Exchange

At this little office, you can speak to the Goblin and purchase a bag of gold galleons. When Muggles buy the gold Galleons however, they are transformed into chocolate!

Dining in Hogsmeade

The original land of Harry Potter at Universal Orlando is the Village of Hogsmeade in Islands of Adventure. Muggles were delighted to get their first taste of butterbeer and other delicacies when the village opened to them in 2010.

The Butterbeer Keg

One place that adds such charm in the Village of Hogsmeade is the big red keg shaped Butterbeer cart. From this cart, cups of Butterbeer, both of the regular variety topped with cream or the frozen variety are served. The line for the Butterbeer Keg can become quite long early in the day. Because of this, a second keg has opened. For a shorter line, perhaps you should order this beverage at the Hog's Head Pub.

Wink: Straws are not offered when purchasing a traditional Butterbeer. A Slytherin wizard placed a hex on the sweet concoction. Knowing Muggles' love of straws, if you attempt to drink your Butterbeer through a straw, it tends to blow up!

The Three Broomsticks

Harry's first taste of Butterbeer was at The Three Broomsticks in Hogsmeade Village. When you step inside this establishment, you'll feel as if you've stepped into the pages of Harry Potter and the Prisoner of Azkaban. This establishment is more than the average quick service theme park restaurant. The hearty menu includes American and British fare to please and satisfy the palate.

When the Harry Potter films were being made, the movie sets of this restaurant were copied from Universal Orlando's designs. The theme is authentic, and don't be surprised if you get a peek of a house elf (or at least its shadow)! The themed atmosphere is so complete, it might distract from your meal.

The Traditional English Breakfast is a feast which can easily feed Hagrid or maybe even two Muggles. It includes eggs, sausage, grilled tomato, bacon, black pudding, potatoes and baked beans. The Americans hate to be outdone. The American breakfast includes eggs, sausage, croissant, potatoes and bacon. Also available is Porridge (oatmeal), Smoked Salmon and pancakes.

Muggles have a habit of visiting theme parks with large families or groups. A menu item fits the bill for a large group. The "Great Feast Platter" which is meant for 4, will probably feed a few more. It includes four full size ears of corn, potatoes, fresh vegetables, ribs and roasted chicken.

The Three Broomsticks Menu

Breakfast Menu

Adults $16.99 / Children $12.39

Traditional English Breakfast
Fresh scrambled eggs, sausage links, black pudding, English

bacon, baked beans, grilled tomato, sautéed mushrooms and breakfast potatoes.

Porridge Breakfast
Old fashioned steamed oats with fresh fruit and butter croissant.

Continental Breakfast
A colorful array of fresh fruit served with croissants accompanied by assorted jams.

American Breakfast
Fresh scrambled eggs, breakfast potatoes, crisp bacon, and link sausage with butter croissant.

Pancake Breakfast
Three fluffy buttermilk pancakes, crisp bacon, and link sausage with butter croissant.

Beverages

Pumpkin Juice™ - $4.99
Hot Tea - $3.29
Fresh Brewed Coffee - $3.29
Apple Juice - $2.69
Orange Juice - $2.69
Milk - $2.99

Lunch And Dinner Menu

The Great Feast

The first course will be a fresh garden salad tossed with our signature vinaigrette dressing. The main course will be a combination of rotisserie smoked chicken & spareribs, corn on the cob, and roast potatoes.
Platter for four - $59.99
Additional serving - $14.99

Main Courses

Fish and Chips - $15.99
Fresh north Atlantic cod battered & fried with chips and tartar sauce.

Shepherd's Pie with Garden Salad - $14.49
Ground beef, lamb & vegetables crowned with potatoes.

Beef Pasties with Garden Salad - $9.99
Flakey pastry pies filled with ground beef, vegetables & potatoes served with a side salad & choice of dressing.

Rotisserie Smoked Chicken Platter - $12.99
Served with corn on the cob and roasted potatoes

Spare Ribs Platter - $16.99
Served with corn on the cob and roasted potatoes

Chicken and Ribs Platter - $15.99
Served with corn on the cob and roasted potatoes

Smoked Turkey Leg - $14.99
Served with wedge fries

Vegetarian Entree
Corn on the cob, roasted potatoes, broccoli

Salads

Salad Dressings
Blue Cheese, Light Italian, Ranch, Thousand Island, Fat Free Ranch

Soup & Salad Combo - $10.49
Leek & Potato or Split Pea Soup, Side salad and choice of dressing

Rotisserie Smoked Chicken Salad - $11.49
Over a bed of fresh greens with choice of dressing

Children's Menu

For ages 9 and under. All meals served with grapes &
applesauce.

Fish & Chips - $6.99
Children's portion includes chips and grapes
Chicken Legs - $6.99
Chicken Fingers - $6.99
Macaroni Cheese - $6.99

Side Items

Garlic Herb Roasted Potatoes - $2.99

Baked Potato - $3.19
Topped with butter & sour cream

Corn on the Cob - $3.99

Seasoned Wedge Fries - $3.49

Fresh Garden Salad - $4.59

Fruit Cup - $3.79

Desserts

Butterbeer™ Ice-Cream - $5.49

Butterbeer™ Potted Cream - $5.79

Cup of Ice-Cream - $4.99
Strawberry and Peanutbutter, Vanilla, or Chocolate

Chocolate Trifle - $3.99
Layered chocolate cake with fresh berries & cream

Beverages

Butterbeer™ (Non-Alcoholic) - $6.99
Frozen Butterbeer™ (Non-Alcoholic) - $6.99
Pumpkin Juice™ - $4.99
Pumpkin Fizz - $4.99
Lemonade - $3.69
Sparkling Water - $3.25
Gillywater - $4.50
Cider (Non-Alcoholic) - $3.69
Apple or Pear
Iced Tea - $3.69
Sweet, Unsweet, Raspberry
Lemonade & Iced Tea Mix - $3.69

Draught Beers

Hog's Head™ Brew - $8.99
Dragon Scale - $8.99

Wink: The Three Broomsticks sign combined with the lantern handing in the center loosely represents the symbol for the Deathly Hallows.

Hog's Head Pub

At the rear of the Three Broomsticks tavern is the Hog's Head Pub. Watch the large stuffed hog's head behind the bar which periodically snarls at guests.

The whole family is welcome in the authentic pub where many enjoy Harry's favorite beverage, Butterbeer. Other drinks include pumpkin juice, lemonade, and cider. Adults can take a seat at the bar and sample the pub's selection of domestic and imported beers, specialty drinks, wine, spirits and mixed drinks including Hagrid's favorite, Fire Whisky.

Hog's Head Pub Beverage Menu

Non-Alcoholic
Butterbeer
Frozen Butterbeer
Pumpkin Juice
Pumpkin Fizz
Lemonade
Sparkling Water
Natural Spring Water
Cider: nonalcoholic apple or pear
Iced Tea: Sweet, Unsweetened, Raspberry
Lemonade and Iced Tea Mix

Alcoholic
Guinness Market Price
Newcastle Market Price
Boddington's Market Price
Stella Artois Market Price
Yeungling Market Price
Miller Lite Market Price
Full Cocktail Menu: Market Price
Hog's Head Brew

Wink: At the Hog's Head, ask for "The Triple," a "secret" drink (formerly referred to as a Deathly Hallows). The drink combines Strongbow Cider, topped with Hog's Head Brew and then topped with Guinness.

The Magic Neep Fruit Cart

The Magic Neep was a magical green grocer in Hogsmeade. At the Wizarding World, local wizards have named the fruit stand in Hogsmeade which sells not only chilled fruit, but also cold drinks, such as water and pumpkin juice, a spiced cold drink with a hint of pumpkin flavour.

Honeydukes

Honeydukes is a shop for the created to tempt wizards' fancy for sweet confections. Dumbledore was one of the shop's best customers, due to his partiality for sweets.

At Honeydukes, Muggles can enjoy all of the Hogwarts students favorite sweets including the ever popular Bertie Bott's Every-Flavour Beans, Exploding Bon Bons, treacle fudge, chocolate cauldrons, cauldron cakes and the coveted Chocolate Frogs.

Magic surrounds these chocolate frogs which have been charmed to melt slowly in the hot Florida weather (however, the charm seems to have backfired because they are so hard that they seem more like Hagrid's rock cakes). Enclosed in each package is an octagon shaped collectible Wizard Trading Card, favored by the magic community.

A note of warning: some of the sweets at Honeydukes have magic surprises such as the popping sensations of Exploding Bon Bons and Fizzing Whisbees. Take care when sampling some of the not so sweet flavours of Bertie Bott's beans!

Popular sweets at Honeydukes (subject to change):

Chocolate Frogs
Bertie Bott's Every Flavour Beans
Clippy's Clip Joint Clippings
Honeydukes Candy Floss
Sugar Quill Lollipop
Honeydukes Milk Chocolate Bar
Pepper Imps
Exploding Bon Bons
Honeydukes Salt Water Taffy
Chocolate Cauldron

Fizzing Whizbees
Honeydukes Hard Candy
Ton-Tongue Toffee

Wizard Trivia Question #25: What kind of sweet from Honeydukes did Ron say burnt a hole through his tongue?

Other Magical Dining Establishments

Just in case you've had enough the crowds of Muggles in Hogsmeade or Diagon Alley, there are a few "magical" places which offer fine dining choices.

Mythos

Adjacent to Hogsmeade is The Lost Continent, a mystical middle eastern land from which Hogsmeade was born (part of the Lost Continent was used to create Hogsmeade). There is a wonderfully magical restaurant voted "best theme park restaurant" for many years in a row. Mythos has a culturally diverse menu featuring gluten free and vegan offerings. The facade features a cascading waterfall from a "wizard's" mouth and trolls can be heard growling under the bridge in the rear near the lake.

Doc Sugrue's Desert Kebab House

Also in the Lost Continent is Doc Surge's Desert Kebab House featuring beef and chicken kebabs and hummus platters.

Fire Eater's Grill

Among the fortune tellers and mystical objects for sale in The Lost Continent is the Fire Eater's Grill. The grill offers American Muggle favorites such as chicken fingers, hot dogs and apple pie as well as gyros and hummus.

Finnegan's Bar & Grill

In the streets of New York, just a short walk through San Francisco from the London Waterfront is Finnegan's Bar & Grill. This Irish pub features a few menu items similar to those found in the Wizarding World, such as Bangers & Mash, Shepherd's Pie, Irish Stew and Fish and Chips.

"The thing about growing up with Fred and George is that you sort of start thinking anything's possible if you've got enough nerve."
Ginny Weasley
Harry Potter and the Half Blood Prince

10 TOURING PLANS

The crafty wizards At universal Orlando have created such a unique opportunity for muggles to experience the magic of the Harry Potter books, and now an overwhelming number of muggles travel from all ends of the earth to experience this phenomenon. In the peak seasons or when a new attraction opens, the number of guests have to be limited due to muggle capacity laws. Alas, the poor muggles are experiencing great frustration due to the crowds.

In my role as Chief Witch of American Muggle Relations, I have created touring guides to assist muggles in the proper procession through the resort for the enhancement of muggle enjoyment. I've created guides for adults, parents with small children, day trips and multiple day trips.

A very important factor to figure into your plans are the season and weather. The "high" season is the busiest times of the year. The high season consists mainly of Summer, but also Christmas, New Years, and Spring Break. The "low" season is in the Fall, Winter and Spring. Because of the popularity of the Wizarding World and the size limits of Diagon Alley, visiting during the low season is the best choice.

Wink: Want to ride Escape from Gringotts but afraid of roller coasters? Well, this ride was designed to be a mild thrill ride! However, there is one drop. Sit in the front row of the cart and by magic, the drop is less steep!

Wink: Check out all of the shops. Each one in the Wizarding World Carries its own unique merchandise. Shopping in Diagon Alley is an attraction itself.

The One-Day Touring Plan

To take advantage of this plan, you must have a park to park ticket. To have the best experience, I recommend touring as early in the morning as you can to avoid crowds.

Arrive at the Universal Studios Florida entrance gate 45 minutes prior to the posted park opening time. If staying onsite, arrive one hour prior to opening time (which means allowing at least 30 minutes for travel on water taxis or shuttles).

• Upon entry, proceed toward New York, then walk through San Francisco and on to the London Waterfront.

• At the London Waterfront, enter Diagon Alley through Leicester Station.

• Prepare to be amazed at entering the world of magic!

• Proceed to Harry Potter and the Escape from Gringotts (look up if you hear the dragon grumbling, to see it breathe fire!)

• Ride Harry Potter and the Escape from Gringotts

• Walk straight to Ollivanders for "The Wand Chooses the Wizard" ceremony and purchase an interactive wand in the shop, or if you're in Slytherin House, you may want to purchase from Wands by Gregorovitch

• Follow the map included with your wand for spell casting

locations throughout Diagon Alley.

• Enter the Carkitt Market area and cast spells or have a Butterbeer at the Hopping Pot while waiting for Celestina Warbeck to perform or catch one of two puppet shows inspired by The Tails of Beedle the Bard.

• On your way to lunch, stroll through Knockturn Alley and visit Borgin and Burkes

• Lunch at The Leaky Cauldron.

• Dessert at Florean Fortescue's Ice Cream Parlour

• Exit Diagon Alley and board the Hogwarts Express to Hogsmeade

• Head to Harry Potter and the Forbidden Journey, check the wait time if more than 50 minutes wait to ride it later when the park is less crowded

• Enjoy a Butterbeer in the Hogs Head Pub (usually a much shorter line than the big keg kiosk). Enjoy the incredible theming in the pub or sit outside on the deck overlooking the lake.

• Spend some time casting spells in the afternoon when the crowds have subsided. Visit the shops such as Honeydukes, and Owl Post (mail a postcard from owl post with the Hogsmeade postmark).

• Ride Harry Potter and the Forbidden Journey. This is one of most popular attractions in Islands of Adventure so ride this in the afternoon when the crowds are lighter. This is two attractions in one: a Hogwarts castle tour and the ride. Take your time touring through the queue so you won't miss anything!

• Flight of the Hippogriff.

• Dinner at the Three Broomsticks. Check the closing time because it closes earlier than the park.

The Two-Day Touring Plan

To take advantage of this plan, you must have a park to park ticket. Arrive at Universal Studios 45 minutes before the posted opening time. If staying onsite, take advantage of Early Park Admission for onsite hotel guests and arrive one hour before the posted park opening time.

Day One

The first stop on your tour depends entirely on whether you would prefer to eat breakfast at the hotel or in Diagon Alley.

• If breakfast is number one on your priority list, head into The Leaky Cauldron for your choice of hearty breakfast platters.

• Make your way to the London Waterfront and enter Diagon Alley.

• Go directly to Harry Potter and the Escape from Gringotts and ride.

• Proceed to Ollivanders for the Wand Chooses the Wizard Ceremony. After the ceremony, you are directed to exit through Ollivander's Wand Shop. Spend some time in the shop, and decide which interactive wand to purchase with the help of Ollivander's staff.

• If it's still breakfast hour or early lunch time, head over to The Leaky Cauldron.

• After a hearty meal is the perfect time to start casting spells.

Use the map included with your wand or download this ebook to your smartphone and follow the chapter on Making Magic. Be sure not to miss the spell locations in Knockturn Alley! You could easily spend hours casting spells and admiring all of the clever details.   Be sure to read the amusing advertisements on the buildings as you walk around.

• Wander through Carkitt Market and be entertained by the talented songstress, Celestina Warbeck and the Banshees or one of the Tales of Beedle the Bard puppet shows.

• At this time, Diagon Alley is probably becoming quite crowded. If the park is open late, now is a good time to go back to your onsite hotel for a rest, a refreshing swim in the hotel pool or a leisurely lunch one of the Muggle restaurants in Universal CityWalk.

• Return to Universal Studios and enter Diagon Alley.

• Enjoy a sweet treat at Florean Fortescue's Ice Cream Parlour.

• Ride the Hogwarts Express from Kings Cross Station to Hogsmeade.

• Enjoy casting spells and sight seeing in Hogsmeade. Hopefully, you'll catch a performance of The Frog Choir or the TriWizard Spirit Rally.

• Ride Flight of the Hippogriff.

• Dinner at The Three Broomsticks.

Day Two

Arrive early 45 minutes early at the entrance to Islands of Adventure or take advantage of Early Park Admission for hotel guests.

- Head to Hogsmeade to ride Harry Potter and the Forbidden Journey. Check out the Marauders Map at Filch's Emporium of Confiscated Goods and browse all the goods for sale on the way out.

- Have breakfast or early lunch at The Three Broomsticks.

- Spend some time casting spells and sight seeing or shopping in Hogsmeade. Be sure to look up to see the Owl clock tower and shop in Honeydukes.

- Ride the Hogwarts Express to Diagon Alley.

- Purchase lunch from The Hopping Pot and have a seat and enjoy a puppet show or musical performance.

- Spend some time in the shops, especially Weasley's Wizard Wheezes, Madame Malkins, and Magical Menagerie

- Have a sweet treat from Florean Fortescue's or enjoy some sweet treats purchased from Sugarplum's. You can also try a magical beverage at The Fountain of Fair Fortune.

- Speak to the Goblin on duty at Gringotts Money Exchange.

- Have a wizard photo shoot at Shutterbuttons.

- Have dinner at The Leaky Cauldron.

11 OTHER "MAGIC" IN THE PARKS

The Wizarding World is not the only magical place found in Universal Orlando. Although performing magic is strictly forbidden by the secrecy statutes set in place by MACUSA (Magical Congress of the United States of America), Universal Orlando is "pushing the envelope."

Although some of these rides display Muggle ingenuity such as engineering marvels like the Incredible Hulk Coaster and the Hollywood Rip Ride Rockit, there are many magical attractions like the two Harry Potter rides, are explained away as "multi-sensory, multi-dimensional." Other rides use Muggle animation talents such as those used on The Simpsons, Shrek and Despicable Me.

All of these aside, wizards and witches know the truth— these are not possible without a little magic! Each of these attractions have had charms placed on them. To the dismay of Universal Orlando executives, MACUSA executives often try to disable these strong charms which explains why the rides sometimes break down!

Magic At Universal Studios

The two most obvious examples of magic found on rides are in three attractions which claim their influence from visitors from other planets—but as all wizards know, the myth of aliens visitors from other planets was created to keep Muggles in the dark about the existence of magical creatures.

E.T. Adventure

An original ride in the park, this ride is about E.T., an extra terrestrial visitor and his quest to get home to heal his planet. This ride is popular with children and nostalgic adults.

MEN IN BLACK Alien Attack

This ride is based on a band of aurors from MACUSA dressed in black who must capture and kill unfriendly "aliens." Instead of wands, guests use "guns" to aim and shoot these magical creatures. Newt Scamander would turn over in his grave to see Muggles being encouraged to kill any magical creatures.

TRANSFORMERS: The Ride-3D

Autobots and evil Decepticons battle in a quest for the Allspark. These creatures bring Muggles on a chase to save Earth as well as a battle of good and evil.

Revenge of the Mummy

Ancient Egypt had a foundation in magic. Dark wizards ruled at the time and Muggles were enraptured with the idea of the magic of the Mummy's power in the afterworld. Muggles are "cursed" as they begin the attraction which turns into an indoor roller coaster. During the attraction, you'll encounter the Mummy, fire, scarab beetles and other dark magic.

Race Through New York Starring Jimmy Fallon

The newest magical attraction uses the magic of the famous wizard, Jimmy Fallon, who entertains Muggles on a daily basis. His attraction takes you on a tour of past wizard hosts of his late night talk show and takes Muggles on a magical ride through New York.

Magic at Islands of Adventure

Most of the attractions at Islands of Adventure have been created by Muggle creativity, but a few are based on magic. There are lands within the park are based on magic. Obviously Marvel Super Hero Island blatantly uses wizards disguised as heroes and villains with "super powers." Another land which displays magic is The Lost Continent which proudly displays magical arts.

The most magical attractions at Islands of Adventure are as follows:

The Amazing Adventures of Spiderman

The famous American auror, Peter Parker, takes on the persona of Spiderman to fight his dark wizard foes who steal the Statue of Liberty.

Poseidon's Fury

This show led by an archeologist is a retelling of the battle between the legendary Lord Darkenon, a famous dark wizard, and Poseidon. Universal wizards created several versions of the aguamenti charm to create special water effects for the show.

Skull Island—Reign of Kong

The fantastic beasts in this attraction were discovered at

about the same time Newt Scamander published his famous textbook. It is believed that creatures such as Kong were created by wizards who tried to create a magical army by embedding the blood of giants into the bodies of wizard friendly apes. King Kong is the result and he's back at Universal. MACUSA was successful in shutting down King Kong's first attraction at Universal Studios, but the King is back and now permanently resides in-between the Toon Lagoon and Jurassic Park areas at Islands of Adventure along with prehistoric creatures and other dangerous magical beasts.

WIZARD TRIVIA ANSWERS

1. When asked his name by Stan Shunpike, the Knight Bus conductor, Harry gave the first name he could think of, Neville Longbottom.

2. On Harry's first visit to Madam Malkin's to be fitted for his wizard robes, he met Draco Malfoy who was also being fitted.

3. At Weasleys Wizard Wheezes, Jenny chose a Pigmy Puff as her magical pet to take to Hogwarts Castle. He is called Harold and is the cause of Crookshanks following Jenny around.

4. When Harry accidentally landed in Borgin & Burkes by way of the Floo Network, he hid in a large black cabinet when the Malfoy's stepped into the shop. This may have been the same "Vanishing Cabinet" which was connected to the one in the "Room of Requirement" which Draco repaired in Harry Potter and the Half Blood Prince.

5. Buckbeak, the Hippogriff, was renamed Witherwings when he was left in Hagrid's care after Sirius Black's death for his protection.

6. The Leaky Cauldron is located on Charing Cross Road in London.

7. One gold Galleon is worth 17 silver Sickles or 493 bronze Knuts. The Galleon was also equivalent to £4.97 GBP, or $10.17 USD.

8. Horned slugs are useful in potions including a potion to treat boils.

9. In the trophy case, on the Gryffindor Quidditch plaque, James Potter is the 1970 Seeker champ. R. J. King was champ in 1969 and M. G. McGonagall was champ in 1971.

10. Hedwig is a snowy owl, sometimes called a "Ghost Owl."

11. Ollivander uses three substances as the magical core to his wands. They are unicorn hair, dragon heartstring and phoenix feather.

12. Albus Dumbledore discovered 12 uses for dragon's blood.

13. Godric Gryffindor, one of the four founders of Hogwarts School of Witchcraft and Wizardry, was the original owner of the Sorting Hat.

14. Moaning Myrtle's full name is Myrtle Elizabeth Warren.

15. Cedric Diggory played seeker and was the captain of the Hufflepuff Quidditch team in his fifth and sixth year.

16. Weasley's Wizard Wheezes is located at 93 Diagon Alley, London, England.

17. The potion known as "Liquid Luck" is Felix Felicis.

18.The vampire who attends Professor Slughorn's party is Sanguini.

19.Tonks' (Nymphadora or as her father calls her, Dora) is the daughter of Andromeda. Her aunts are Narcissa Malfoy and Bellatrix Lestrange. Her cousin is Draco Malfoy.

20.Essence of Dittany is known and used for its extremely effective healing properties.

21.Like the Dark Lord, Dolores Umbridge is a half blood witch, whose middle name is Jane.

22.The Sword of Gryffindor is encrusted with Rubies, the same stones which represent Gryffindor House at Hogwarts is the hourglass that counts the house points.

23.Harry was with Ron and Hermione at the Three Broomsticks when he overheard Minister Fudge say that not only were Sirius and James Potter best friends, but that Lily and James had named Sirius as Harry's Godfather.

24.Hagrid brought Harry chocolate and raspberry ice cream on his first visit to Diagon Alley while he was being fitted for school robes.

25.Ron told Harry that when he was seven, Fred gave him an Acid Pop and it burnt a hole right through his tongue. Mrs. Weasley then walloped Fred with her broomstick.

AUTHOR'S NOTES

As a born and bred "Cajun," I grew up surrounded by the folklore of the swamps of Louisiana. As a child, stories of "The Loup Garou" enchanted and scared me and the legend of displaced lovers in Longfellow's poem, Evangeline, captivated my spirit. In Louisiana, there is a rich Native American heritage with is reflected in names nearby my home such as Houma, Choctaw and Coushatta. There has always been a mysticism associated with the legends of Native Americans.

As I grew into adulthood, I often traveled to the state of Florida on family vacations, visiting the white sand beaches and the emerald water of the gulf of Mexico. I first visited Walt Disney World at a young age which started a life long love of Orlando theme parks.

As a Harry Potter geek, I was a late bloomer. At the urging of my son, I read all seven books of the Harry Potter series by J. K. Rowling and was hooked! I watched all the movies and opened a Pottermore account. After all of this prep, I couldn't have been more excited at the prospect of visiting The Wizarding World of Harry Potter by Universal Orlando.

Many people ask me about my inspiration for writing a travel guide with a fictional character who narrates the guide. I wanted a strong female voice in my writing and I thought J. K. Rowling would appreciate a high ranking female in the Magical Congress.

My idea for writing this guide was sparked when I came up with the notion of an American witch introducing Muggles to the wizarding world at Universal Orlando (this was long before the announcement of the film, Fantastic Beasts and Where to Find Them). I wanted my witch to have roots in mysticism. This led me to decide that the witch should be Native American. My original thought for her name was Marietta Blackwater. I came up with the last name, Blackwater, because I remembered a visit to the Blackwater State Park near Destin, Florida. The state of Florida was ideal because in it, there is not only Orlando, but also the legend of the Fountain of Youth and other mysticisms.

I liked the name Marietta because it is a version of my own name and there is a character named Marietta Edgecombe in Harry Potter and the Order of the Phoenix. She was Cho Chang's best friend but also the student who betrayed Dumbledore's Army to Professor Umbridge. I couldn't let my American Ambassador's name have such an affiliation.

On my next trip to Florida, while traveling east on Interstate 10, I passed an exit for a town called Marianna and I knew instantly that my witch's name should be Marianna Blackwater.

I like the idea of offering a different point of view than most travel guides offer. I wanted to tell a story and encourage readers imagination. I hope readers notice all the details of magic and encourage their own sense of creativity when touring the theme parks. I also hope to foster generations of guests to keep reading these books and encourage their children to imagine the miracles of magic.

Thank you for reading my travel guide and I hope you have many great trips to The Wizarding World of Harry Potter at Universal Orlando.

ABOUT THE AUTHOR

Mary deSilva is a Muggle from Louisiana. She is an author, acrylic painting and glass artist, teacher, chef and avid traveler. At the insistence of her son, she read all seven Harry Potter books back to back, watched all of the movies, and created her own Pottermore account. She is now a self-proclaimed "Harry Potter Geek." She has published seven Orlando travel books available on Amazon Kindle.

For more information, Facebook: @MaryDesilvaAuthor
Follow on Instagram: @maryfdesilva
YouTube channel: CajunDIYDiva
Artwork can be found at FineArtAmerica.com
DestinationsDiva.blogspot.com

Made in the USA
Monee, IL
13 April 2020